FLEETWOOD MAC

Rumours n' Fax

BY ROY CARR AND STEVE CLARKE

FLEETWOOD MAC
Rumours n' Fax

HARMONY BOOKS/NEW YORK

Dedication

*To whom it may concern—
past, present and future!*

**Book and Cover Design
by Janet Sutherland**

Published simultaneously in Canada by General
Publishing Co., Ltd.
Printed in the United States of America

**Library of Congress Cataloging
In Publication Data**

Carr, Roy
　　Fleetwood Mac: Rumours 'n fax.

　　1. Fleetwood Mac (musical quintet) Clarke,
Steve I., joint author.
ML421.F57C4　　784'.092'2　　78-2475
ISBN 0-517-53364-2
ISBN 0-517-53365-0 pbk.

Acknowledgments

The authors wish to express their gratitude to
the following friends and organizations for
their co-operation in the writing of this book:

Mick Fleetwood, Bob Welch, Mike Vernon,
Claude Nobs, Louis Raynor, the lovely Moira
Bellas and the super-efficient staff of WEA
Records' London Press office, especially
David the Rave, Dave the Monster, Brian,
Angela, Steve, Franco, Graham, Neil and
Jackie. Likewise, Julia, Elly, Jonathan and
Simon of CBS Records' London Press office,
and Jane McKibben, Hugh Collingwood, Paul
McNally, Sire Records.

Tom Ruffino, Marilyn Moore, Nick Logan,
Lois Marino, Barbara Goldstein, David
Hughes, Debbie Bennett, Fred Dove, Fran
Papier, Tony Tyler, Kate Phillips, Beverly
Ballard, Pete Frame, Barry "Wipeout"
Appleby and Ted Carroll of *Rock On*
(London), Roy Day, Ken Muis, Mike and Pete of
Vintage Records (London), Didy Lake, Wendy
Gilliatt, Judy Wong, David Wedgeberry, Jon
Donaldson, Cheerful Charlie Webster,
Michael Grey, Judy Riley, Bill "Foxy" Fowler,
Geoff "Grumpy" Grimes, Flyover Records,
Gary Kenton, Kim Clarke, and Bruce Harris,
David Bain, Manuela Soares, Janet Suther-
land and Murray Schwartz.

New Musical Express, Billboard, DJM
Records, Decca Records, NEMS Records,
Bleeker Bob's Oldies Shop (Greenwich
Village).

The Palace Hotel, Montreux, Switzerland,
the Continental Hyatt House, Hollywood,
California, the Beverly Wilshire Hotel,
Hollywood, California, St. Regis Hotel, New
York, and the Harbour Castle, Toronto,
Canada.

**Thanks also to the following for the
photographs:**

Bob Baker, Adrian Boot, Paul Canty, Clutton
Photos, Fin Costello, Andre Csillag, Nate
Cutler (Globe Photos), Chalkie Davies,
Decca Records, DJM Records, Flair Photos
Limited, H. Goodwin, Mel Grundy, David Hill,
Alan Johnson, London Features International,
London Photo Agency, Janet Macoska, Lynn
McAfee, *New Musical Express,* Photo Trends,
Pictorial Press, Barry Plummer, Michael
Putland, Roger Ressmeyer, Retna, *Rolling
Stone* (Annie Liebowitz), Julian Ruthven, SKR
Photos International, Joseph Stevens, Syndica-
tion International, David Wainwright, Chris
Walter, George Wilkes, Words & Faces, and
Richard Young.

Front cover: Adrian Boot

Back cover: Barry Plummer

Color section: Fin Costello (Retna), Lynn
McAfee, Michael Putland (Retna), and Roger
Ressmeyer (Retna).

Contents

Most newspapers employ scribes whose sole function is regularly to update the unpublished obituaries of prominent personalities. But it would take scores of full time researchers to keep abreast of the fluctuating fortunes of Fleetwood Mac—the band that continues to exist despite itself.

In the eleven years since Fleetwood Mac debuted at the height of Flower Power on August 12, 1967, at Great Britain's National Blues & Jazz Festival at Windsor, the band has transmogrified from a star-crossed guitar-hero-dominated blues outfit into one of the world's biggest-ever album-sellers: its "Rumours" LP stayed at the top of the American chart longer than any other rock album in music industry history—in excess of six consecutive months.

But it has been a career continually fraught with impending disaster. Guitarists have quit under harrowing banner headlines, bogus lineups have laid claim to the name, and those original members who stuck it out have enacted more melodramas than cynical soap opera scriptwriters could concoct in a lifetime of weekly episodes. In truth, all aspects of human emotion are to be found in Fleetwood Mac.

As founder member/drummer Mick Fleetwood so blithely puts it, "being in Fleetwood Mac is more like being in group therapy," adding, "this band may bring out the weak points in a person's character, but by the very same token it strengthens others." Bassist John

McVie feels that comparisons with *Mary Hartman* are equally appropriate.

Bands have broken up for much less, but Fleetwood Mac stubbornly refuses to roll over and expire. Call it masochistic, but the band appears to thrive on one Big Hurt after another.

Up until the middle of 1976, Fleetwood Mac had resigned themselves to the fact that they worked to live, lived to work, and, unlike many of their contemporaries, weren't in a position to rest up for a year or three to rethink, record or contemplate the mysteries of the universe.

Their albums almost always got reviewed, made brief, though inauspicious appearances in the best sellers, and received more air time than some records enjoying healthier sales returns.

It may not have been La Dolce Vita, but at least the bar bill got paid.

The Bluesbreakers: John Mayall, John McVie, Hughie Flint, and Eric Clapton.

STUDIO '51
10/11 GT. NEWPORT STREET
LEICESTER SQUARE (Tube)

Rhythm and Blues

Friday, 8.0
JOHN MAYALL Blues Breakers

Sunday, 4 until 6.30
THE ROLLING STONES

Monday, 8.0
JOHN MAYALL Blues Breakers

In the beginning (or as far as Fleetwood Mac were concerned), there was the Word and the Word was *blues*. Although this ethnic black American music had been fermenting on the British club scene since the dawn of the '60s (and before), it had quickly lost its initial purity with the advent of Beatlemania and the ensuing stampede by British beat groups for the Almighty Dollar.

With the Rolling Stones, Manfred Mann, Spencer Davis, the Animals and the Yardbirds synthesizing the basic form for chart consumption, there were only two people still performing on the British club circuit who hadn't seemingly bastardized the blues.

Neither could be termed *teen fodder*.

There was the nasal hyena howl of an eccentric Mancunian treehouse dweller, Mr. John Mayall, and the cultured growl of one Alexis Korner. Both were much respected founding fathers whose volatile bands acted as incubators for innumerable aspiring soloists. A third British Blues Big Daddy, harp blower Cyril Davies, had died in 1964, a victim of leukemia at the age of 32.

Though The Rolling Stones had topped the British singles chart towards the end of 1964 with an ethnically daring version of Willie Dixon's "Little Red Rooster," grassroots urban blues was still only a minority cult.

The record responsible for opening the floodgates was "Blues Breakers," John Mayall's second album, on which he uncharacteristically shared the billing with his guitarist at the time, Eric Clapton.

In an act of extraordinary idealism, and some would say naivete, Clapton had put musical integrity before commercial excess, when the year before, in 1965, he had publicly denounced and quit the Yardbirds for blatantly compromising their original blues stance (by recording Graham Gouldham's pop-oriented "For Your Love").

"Bluesbreakers" was the first _classic_ British blues album. It consolidated Clapton's reputation as guitarist célèbre, and ushered in the age of the guitar hero. It also gave the British blues movement commercial impetus, staying on the album charts for three months—unprecedented for a blues LP.

Eric Clapton might have been the focal point of the Bluesbreakers, but on occasion the group's bassist John McVie would grab some of the limelight by crashing backwards into his speaker-stack, a willing victim of the great god Bacchus. A former tax officer trainee, McVie was introduced to the blues-wailing Mayall in 1963 by another bassist, the late Cliff Barton, former lynchpin for Cyril Davies and British R & B pioneer Georgie Fame. It was baptism by fire for the 16-year-old. "It was a terrifying experience," McVie once recalled. "John Mayall said 'Right, play a 12-bar,' and I said, 'what's a 12-bar?'"

The blues, all 12 bars of it, was not in the curriculum of the smart stepping Shadows type groups in which McVie had done his basic training. Mayall, true to his Northern roots, had no time for subtleties. "He just gave me a pile of records," said McVie, "and asked me to listen to them and try to grasp the style and feeling."

With four years' service in Mayall's ever-changing ranks, McVie might still be there today, were it not that a relatively unknown guitarist, Peter Green, stepped into the unenviable spot vacated by the Cream-bound Clapton in July 1966.

Eric Clapton, guitarist of heroic proportions, during a Bluesbreakers session.

Introduction

Within a year or so, London East Ender Green (real name Greenbaum) had, after initial public resentment, shaken off Clapton's mantle, established himself as every bit as fine a blues player as Clapton, and taken McVie and drummer Mick Fleetwood from under Mayall's autocratic wing to form Fleetwood Mac—though at first McVie was reluctant to leave the security of the Bluesbreakers.

While McVie had known few employers other than Mayall, Green and Fleetwood were hardened veterans of the road. Between July 1963 and April 1965, Fleetwood drummed for the Cheynes (previously the Senders), a London-based band who blatantly billed themselves as "Britain's Most Exciting Rhythm & Blues Sound."

The Cheynes were formed by a precocious young organist called Peter Bardens, an ambitious, some would say arrogant lad who later worked alongside Van Morrison in Them and Rod Stewart in Shotgun Express. Today, Bardens earns his keep with the low-profile techno-flashers group, Camel.

Typically, Fleetwood joined the Cheynes more by accident than intent. The gangling youth had hitherto confined his artistry to lone sessions in the family Notting Hill Gate garage. A chance meeting between Fleetwood's sister and Bardens resulted in the 15-year-old drummer quitting his job at Liberty's (a London department store) and joining the Cheynes.

All that remains of the Cheynes are three singles, of which only "Stop Running Around" (the B-side of their last single) continues to attract attention by proxy. The song was written by Rolling Stones' bassist Bill Wyman after the Cheynes had accompanied the Stones on their second British tour a year earlier.

When, in April 1965, Bardens disbanded the Cheynes to join Them, Fleetwood drifted into the Bo Street Runners, whose only claim to fame was that they had won television's *Ready Steady Go* beat group competition. "When I joined," Fleetwood recounts, "the Bo Street Runners were already on their way out."

The drummer did stay long enough to cut one single, "Baby Never Say Goodbye," before reuniting with Bardens, on the rebound from Them, to form a new band in February 1966.

Peter B's Looners (soon truncated to Peter Bees) was purely an instrumental quartet unashamedly modelled on the Stax Records' house band, Booker T and the MGs. Bardens' brainchild lasted less than four months, still sufficient time to cut a rework of Jimmy Soul's "If You Wanna Stay Happy," and for Fleetwood to pal up with the group's 18-year-old guitarist Peter Green, who'd previously bashed around on bass and guitar with local sock-hop nonentities like the Tridents and the Muskrats.

Three months later, after adding vocalists Rod Stewart and Beryl Marsden, the group metamorphosized into Shotgun Express. A pale imitation of Stewart's previous outfit (Steampacket), Fleetwood and Green were backing a loser.

Two dead end singles ("I Could Feel The Whole World Turn Round" and "Funny Cos Neither Could I") and the group's lack of professionalism meant that they were stuck with trudging around Britain's Northern Soul Clubs.

Green was smart enough to quit Shotgun

Opposite page: *John McVie handles bass during a session shortly before deserting Mayall in favor of Fleetwood Mac.* Above: *Mayall's band's best (see discography on page 117).*

Express after just two months to join John Mayall. Mick Fleetwood remained until the band committed professional suicide nine months after conception.

While Green's erstwhile colleague Fleetwood was temporarily employed as a decorator, the guitarist was laying down the groundwork for Fleetwood Mac on John Mayall's "A Hard Road" album.

On replacing Clapton, the sensitive Green quickly overreacted to audience shouts of "Bring back Eric" by asserting his normally mild personality in an overbearing way. Though every bit as good a player as Clapton, he felt the need to "big-time." Three years later, Green was to overreact again, this time, however, with a severe bout of humility.

The guitar Green played with Mayall was in the "closer-to-B. B. King-than-thou" purist style. In fact, B. B. King himself admitted to the authors that Green was "the only living guitarist to make me sweat. He's got the sweetest tone I've ever heard."

Whereas Clapton might occasionally throw in a lick for pure effect, Green never showed any hint of these maverick urges. Where one guitarist would play five notes, Green would floor them with a single shot. This economy of style is comparable to some of trumpeter Miles Davis' work with the late John Coltrane.

The sound Green used to coax out of his mutilated Gibson Les Paul (he had removed the top pickup) possessed none of the rock influence of Clapton's harsher tone. Unlike Clapton, Green was not averse to a soupçon of reverb on his amplifier, another B. B. King trick.

Considering Mayall's notorious autocracy and Green's lack of any track record, the latter's contribution to "A Hard Road" was surprising. Not only did Green grab the vocal spotlight on one song, his own composition "The Same Way," he also had two instrumentals pretty much to himself. One of these, the sinister "The Supernatural," another self-penned opus, is a precursor of Fleetwood Mac's biggest-ever British hit "Albatross."

"A Hard Road" was released in Britain in February 1967. Eight weeks later, Fleetwood temporarily replaced Mayall's drummer Aynsley Dunbar, who'd joined uppity Jeff Beck's group. "It was never a serious long-term venture in my mind," admits Fleetwood, "which was just as well, because I was asked to leave after a month."

Seemingly, Mayall could turn a blind eye to McVie's tippling, but having the entire rhythm section legless didn't amuse "The Father of the British Blues," as Mayall had been dubbed. As things turned out, Fleetwood and Green were reunited just two months later in "Peter Green's Fleetwood Mac."

On leaving Mayall, it seems, Green was unsure of his immediate future; one report suggests the young guitarist was planning a pilgrimage to Chicago's South Side to work alongside the city's bluesmen. Others state that Green had absolutely no intention of forming his own unit.

However, producer Mike Vernon thinks that, in collusion with McVie and Fleetwood, the guitarist had been for some time secretly plotting a mass walkout from underneath Mayall's thumb. Some go as far as to say that Mayall encouraged the trio's mutiny.

Vernon himself, disenchanted with his salaried role as a Decca house producer, harbored ambitions of expanding his hither-to low-key specialist Blue Horizon record label into a full-blown concern.

To achieve this, Vernon and his brother Richard needed the pressing and distribution facilities of a major company. Decca was interested, but not in granting label identity, so Vernon sought an alternative outlet, and a deal was signed with CBS.

As self-confessed blues purists, Green, McVie, and Fleetwood reckoned that Blue Horizon would have the right kind of ethnic credibility for their own venture. Indeed, in March 1967, the three (minus Mayall) had laid down tracks with American blues star Eddie Boyd for Vernon's cult label.*

The name "Fleetwood Mac" had first manifested itself as the title of a Bluesbreakers' instrumental jam recorded in 1967, but not unearthed until 1971 on "The Original Fleetwood Mac" album.

Though "Peter Green's Fleetwood Mac" is derived from the names of its three founder members, Green was anxious to recruit a second lead guitarist.

Enter Jeremy Spencer, clutching "The Best Of Elmore James" (the late Mississippi blues legend who exerted a profound influence on British blues) and a copy of the first Cliff Richard album.

To say that Spencer (who looked like an anemic elf) was besotted with Elmore James is

*During the period Fleetwood Mac were under contract to Blue Horizon Records, the group occasionally acted as either house band or featured sidemen on sessions fronted by other label mates: Otis Spann, Eddie Boyd, Duster Bennett, Gordon Smith, Martha Valez, Rod Stewart. They also did sessions with Bob Brunning's Sunflower Band on the budget Saga label.

Opposite page: *Mayall with his group: Peter Green, Hughie Flint, and John McVie.* Above: *"A Hard Road" appeared before Mick Fleetwood arrived on the scene. He didn't last long (see discography on page 117).*

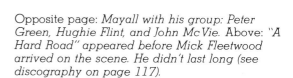

Introduction

The Windsor Festival showcased a stunning array of talent— including a new group with the initials "F.M."

BALLOON MEADOW
A newly designed site
at The Royal
WINDSOR
Racecourse
Maidenhead Rd. (A308)

7TH NATIONAL
JAZZ·POP·BALLADS &
BLUES FESTIVAL

An NJF/MARQUEE preśentation
Sponsored by THE EVENING NEWS

Friday 11th August   **8—11.30 pm**
Tickets 12/6

SMALL FACES THE MOVE
The Nite People · The Syn
THE MARMALADE · Tomorrow

JAZZ & POP

Saturday 12th August   **2.30—5.30 pm**
Tickets 7/6

JEANNIE LAMBE · DANNY MOSS
Mike Carr Trio with Harold McNair
Graham Collier Septet
& FROM THE U.S.A. YUSEF LATEEF
ZOOT SIMS & AL COHN

PAUL JONES
Richard Kent Style

Saturday 12th August   **7—11.30 pm**
Tickets 15/-

THE PINK FLOYD
ZOOT MONEY · AMEN CORNER · TIME BOX
The Crazy World of ARTHUR BROWN · 10 Years After
Aynsley Dunbar Retaliation · ADAMS Recital

For Special
PARTY RATES
and all enquiries
contact the
NJF secretary
at the
MARQUEE
GER 0001

Sunday 13th August   **2.30—5.30 pm**
Tickets 7/6

DONOVAN
OTTILIE PATTERSON
John Slaughter Trio
Al Stewart · Picadilly Line

Why not make a weekend of it?
Stay at our beautiful riverside
CAMP SITE
Bring your own tent etc
We provide water, toilets and
shop. For details contact NJF secretary

BALLADS & BLUES

TRAVEL: By road turn
off M4 at Windsor/Eton
Bypass. Thames Valley
Green Line and London
Country Buses. Western
& Southern Region Trains
SPECIAL LATE service
to Staines, Twickenham,
Richmond, Clapham and
Waterloo.

THE CREAM
JEFF BECK · P. P. ARNOLD · ALAN BOWN
JOHN MAYALL · Chicken Shack · Blossom Toes

Sunday 13th August   **7—11.30 pm**
Tickets 15/-

Debut of
PETER GREEN'S
Fleetwood Mac

The Pentangle with
BERT JANSCH

DENNY
LAINE
strings

an understatement. Until he heard James singing "The Sun Is Shining" (later recorded by Mac as the B-side of "Black Magic Woman") Spencer had no time for blues. Afterwards, he was a changed man.

The diminutive Spencer was a Mike Vernon discovery. He'd come across Spencer in a Birmingham-based blues group, The Levi Set, a band whose only saving grace was, according to Vernon, the childlike Spencer. The Levi Set failed a Decca/Blue Horizon audition, but Spencer was just what Green had in mind to complete Mac's ranks.

With a front line of Green and Spencer, Fleetwood Mac were all set to introduce themselves to the public when John McVie got cold feet, and decided to remain for the moment in the relative security of Mayall's Bluesbreakers. One Bob Brunning was strongarmed into the band while McVie mulled things over. He'd seen Fleetwood Mac at their Windsor debut (as Mayall was on the same bill) and hadn't been impressed, going so far as to say he found them "boring."

Brunning, who'd known all along that his stay was purely temporary, was ousted in McVie's favor in September. The stray bassist formed his own blues group the Brunning Sunflower Band; they recorded three albums for Saga.

While Fleetwood remembers Mac's debut at Windsor as "auspicious," no one could have imagined what Fate had in store.

If they had, McVie might still be with Mayall.*

*Recently, John McVie guested on John Mayall's "Banquet of Blues" album.

14

Stevie
Nicks

Christine McVie

Lindsey Buckingham

John McVie

Mick Fleetwood

In Concert

The History of FLEETWOOD MAC

PETER GREEN'S FLEETWOOD MAC

(A) I Believe My Time Ain't Long (James) Jeremy Spencer vocal/**(B) Rambling Pony** (Green) Peter Green vocal

Produced: Mike Vernon.
(US) Not released. (UK) Blue Horizon 3051.
Released: November 3, 1967.

Even though Peter Green's name is most prominent on the group's masthead, it is left to the only unbilled member, Jeremy Spencer, to introduce the group to the record-buying public.

Typically, Spencer chose a number by his Mississippi avatar, the late Elmore James' "I Believe My Time Ain't Long," itself a hand-me-down from legendary '30s blues mysterioso Robert Johnson's "I Believe I'll Dust My Broom."

In keeping with their purist stance, Fleetwood Mac's interpretation of James' arrangement makes no overt concessions to commerciality. The performance is gloriously spontaneous, the sound infectiously raw, Fleetwood Mac personalizing other peoples' licks with alchemistic flair.

Whereas John Mayall's interpretations of sacrosanct blues standards sometimes veered towards the dour, Fleetwood Mac had the ability to inject a sense of both fun and commitment into the proceedings.

Spencer's nimble bottleneck guitar slips 'n' slides along the fret board with greased ease, Green punctuates the mid-tempo 12-bar shuffle with excellent harmonica breaks, while John McVie and Mick Fleetwood tie the knot for what will become a lengthy rhythmic relationship.

Hip record buyers were already more than acquainted with the B-side, essentially a spartan version of Cream's no-holds-barred rock and roll treatment of Muddy Waters' "Rollin' and Tumblin'," which had appeared the previous year on the power trio's debut album, "Fresh Cream." Using classic blues imagery, Green had rewritten the lyric (an accepted practice in blues circles); hence the title change.

A fast heartbeat drum throbs throughout while a solitary guitar and harmonica repeat the primitive riff. The lead vocal and accompanying background moan is reminiscent of a traditional Deep South plantation field holler.

Inaugurating Blue Horizon's tie-up with CBS, initial copies of this single were sold in a blue and white picture sleeve, with the motto, printed under the joint, "Really The Blues" logos.

Opposite page: *Mick Fleetwood, Peter Green, John McVie, and Jeremy Spencer were the original Fleetwood Mac. Below: The first Fleetwood Mac single, "Really the Blues," came out on the Blue Horizon label in 1967.*

Jeremy Spencer, Mick Fleetwood, Peter Green, and John McVie ham it up for the camera.

PETER GREEN'S FLEETWOOD MAC
PETER GREEN'S FLEETWOOD MAC

Produced: Mike Vernon.
(US) Epic BN.26402. Released: June 3, 1968.
(UK) Blue Horizon 63200. Released: February 24, 1968. Re-released: CBS/Embassy 31036. October 5, 1973.

My Heart Beat Like a Hammer (Spencer) Jeremy Spencer vocal/ **Merry Go Round** (Green) Peter Green vocal/ ***Long Grey Mare** (Green) Peter Green vocal/ **Hellhound On My Trail** (Trad arr: Green) Jeremy Spencer vocal/ **Shake Your Moneymaker** (James) Jeremy Spencer vocal/ **Looking For Somebody** (Green) Peter Green vocal/ **No Place To Go** (Burnett) Peter Green vocal/ **My Baby's Good To Me** (Spencer) Jeremy Spencer vocal/ **I Loved Another Woman** (Green) Peter Green vocal/ **Cold Black Night** (Spencer)

Jeremy Spencer vocal/ **The World Keeps On Turning** (Green) Peter Green vocal/ **Got To Move** (Williamson) Jeremy Spencer vocal

Personnel:
Peter Green (vocal, guitar, harmonica), Jeremy Spencer (vocal, guitar, piano), John McVie (bass), Mick Fleetwood (drums). *Bob Brunning (bass).

From the outset, Peter Green was determined not to deviate from his plan. "There were," he insisted, "a million groups making a mockery of the blues. And a million guitarists playing as fast as they could and calling it blues. I didn't want the music messed about with." His tone was adamant. "I was possessive about it."

True to his words, the music contained on "Fleetwood Mac" reeked of ethnic credibility, cover artwork and all.

It was common for American blues albums to carry either a stylized photograph of the artist (if they were photogenic), a big-legged Mama, a stumblebum taking the air along skid row or a downtrodden back-porch scenario. Fleetwood Mac plumped for a still life of trashcans and a local hellhound (obviously on the trail!).

Fostering no illusions of their "popability," the group confined action-packed mugshots to the back cover.

Music was the message, ma'an.

Material-wise, Green's credited with six songs, though in fact "Hellhound On My Trail" is Robert Johnson's work, and not, as credited, traditional. Spencer weighs in with three songs, each of them owing more than a passing nod to E. James Esq., while James himself and fellow veterans Howlin' Wolf (a.k.a. Chester Burnett) and Sonny Boy

Williamson (Rice Miller) mop up the rest.

Musicologists might like to note that Wolf's "No Place To Go" was to appear two years later on yet another important debut album, "Led Zeppelin," this time bearing a titanium overcoat and new composer credits.

Unlike Cream (then at their zenith), Fleetwood Mac's reading of the blues text was at this stage totally devoid of all rock influence. Whereas Eric Clapton and Jimi Hendrix, encouraged by hallucinogenics, had long since jettisoned the ethnic grace of their original mentors, Green had no truck with psychedelic pyrotechnics.

Over the years, an illusion has grown that Fleetwood Mac was Peter Green's band. As this album retrospectively reveals, this was not so. Green was not the all-embracing dominating figurehead; it wasn't Green and then more Green. The rest of the group weren't subservient shadows, even if, in these formative years, Green was responsible for Mac's more enduring statements.

Moreover, on this album at any rate, Green plays more harp than guitar—the instrument for which he's celebrated. Only twice is Green's electric guitar prowess showcased to any effect on this LP; on "Merry-Go-Round," a slow-burning B.B. King evocation as sweet and tender as any lover's caress, and on "I Loved Another Woman," sensual sophistication enhanced with icy reverb and a quasi-bossa nova backbeat. Santana's adaptation of Green's "Black Magic Woman" owes more to this track than to the original.

Jeremy Spencer had a field day in his guise as the ghost of Elmore James. Spencer had one lick and he sure as hell made the most of it. Derivative it was, but Spencer's zest and

affection transcended the self-imposed limitations—that, and the group's collective magic. The only time Spencer eschewed his love for the Mississippi Marvel was on Johnson's "Hellhound On My Trail," which features the Boy Wonder on primitive piano.

If one track can be said to encapsulate the sheer overriding force of this band it's "Shake Your Moneymaker." As you might guess, an Elmore James song with Spencer out front busting a gut, while his colleagues swing like the proverbial dog's hind leg.

Though according to its producer Mike

"There were millions of groups making a mockery of the blues," said Peter Green of the music scene back in 1968—but Peter Green's Fleetwood Mac wasn't one of them.

Peter Green, 1968.

Vernon, this album only took three days to make, one track "Long Grey Mare" (and Green wasn't singing about horses!) stems from an earlier period.

As already mentioned, before John McVie joined The Mac, Bob Brunning was summoned at the 13th hour as a temporary replacement for the hesitant McVie. "Long Grey Mare," a staccato riff number, appears to be the only known documentation of Brunning's brief residency.

If Mac's debut single, "I Believe My Time Ain't Long," had failed to capture the public imagination, this album struck with a vengeance. No less than 17 weeks in the Top Ten (at one point reaching the No. 4 slot), it went on to accrue 13 months on the British best-selling album charts, and, in terms of vinyl popularity placed Fleetwood Mac in the Beatles and Rolling Stones bracket.

Elmore James never saw it like this!

FLEETWOOD MAC

(A) Black Magic Woman (Green) Peter Green vocal/ **(B) The Sun Is Shining** (James) Jeremy Spencer vocal

Produced: Mike Vernon.
(US) Not released. (UK) Blue Horizon 3138.
Released: March 29, 1968.

Bluesmen—black and white—have always been obsessed with images of the devil; witness Robert Johnson's harrowing "Me And The Devil Blues," the lyric of which is so vivid that it gave vent to the rumor that Johnson *had* in fact sold his soul to the devil.

And for Fleetwood Mac's second single, Peter Green adopted the blues legacy of personifying the devil as *femme fatale*. Obviously less disturbing than the luckless Johnson's song, Green's "Black Magic Woman" was nevertheless a potent brew.

Released (in the UK) just four weeks after Mac's chartbusting debut album, and still retaining the same basic 12-bar structure, albeit with some sneaky time jiggery-pokery, "Black Magic Woman" exudes style and confidence.

Having personalized traditional modes, with this single Fleetwood Mac flex a collective bicep and come on really heavy. Mick Fleetwood's penchant for stylish though not fancy *voodoo* tomtom work, coupled with Green's recurring sustained sinister single note, conjure up a sultry mood.

Like most classic rock singles (and this *is* a rock single), "Black Magic Woman" clocks in under three minutes, still more than enough time for Green to turn his attention away from the microphone (where he does a sterling job) to lay down two choruses of some of 1968's most imaginative guitar playing.

Despite its excellence, "Black Magic Woman" failed to stun the charts, and it was left to former blade-carrying Mexican guitarist Carlos Santana to turn Green's song into a world-wide million seller. We hasten to add that though Santana's version is not without its merits, it nevertheless lacks the blues bite of the original.

Elmore James is yet again represented by Jeremy Spencer, though this time in a much less convincing mood, and on the B-side.

Seemingly Spencer's notorious sense of humor gets the better of him on this tortured and tortuous dirge.

Elmore James never saw it like this either!

FLEETWOOD MAC

(A) Black Magic Woman (Green) Peter Green
vocal/ (B) Long Grey Mare (Green) Peter Green
vocal

Produced: Mike Vernon.
(US) Epic 5-10351. Released: June 7, 1968.
(UK) Not released.

Obviously, someone in Epic's New York office
wasn't an Elmore James fan and so a different
B-side was assigned.

FLEETWOOD MAC

(A) Need Your Love So Bad (John) Peter Green
vocal/(B) Stop Messin' 'Round (Green, Adams)
Peter Green vocal

Produced: Mike Vernon.
(US) Not released. (UK) Blue Horizon 3139.
Released: July 5, 1968.

Peter Green decided to record "Need Your
Love So Bad" after his former employer John
Mayall had played him a live version of the
song by Green's mentor, American blues
guitar supremo B.B. King.

In a respectful effort to emulate the style
King was moving into, Green recruited the
services of guitarist-arranger Mickey Baker
(of Mickey & Sylvia "Love Is Strange" fame) to
score the string accompaniment.

A slow minor key reflective blues, Green's
beautifully restrained voice and guitar obbli-
gato are juxtaposed with Baker's equally
tasteful backdrop to produce a twilight mood
of velvet sophistication.

Ironically enough, considering its low profile, "Need Your Love So Bad" gave Fleetwood
Mac their first, though extremely brief, flirtation with the British singles chart.

At least someone out there had taste.

In complete contrast, the B-side (a foretaste
of Mac's imminent second LP "Mr. Wonderful") is a carousing knockabout boogie shuffle
replete with bar-room piano, sandpaper horns
and frenetic fretboarding. Not surprisingly, it
was all about woman trouble.

Above: *Fleetwood and McVie in close
consultation.* Above right: *The Woburn festival
had a heavy lineup.*

A younger Mick Fleetwood back in 1968.

MR. WONDERFUL
FLEETWOOD MAC

Produced: Mike Vernon.
(US) Not released. (UK) Blue Horizon 63205.
Released: August 23, 1968.

Stop Messin' 'Round (Green, Adams) Peter Green vocal/I've Lost My Baby (Spencer) Jeremy Spencer vocal/Rollin' Man (Green, Adams) Peter Green vocal/Dust My Broom (Johnson) Jeremy Spencer vocal/Love That Burns (Green, Adams) Peter Green vocal/ Doctor Brown (Brown) Jeremy Spencer vocal/Need Your Love Tonight (Spencer) Jeremy Spencer vocal/If You Be My Baby (Green, Adams) Peter Green vocal/Evenin' Boogie (Spencer) Instrumental/Lazy Poker Blues (Green, Adams) Peter Green vocal/Coming Home (James) Jeremy Spencer vocal/Trying Hard To Forget (Green, Adams) Peter Green vocal

Personnel:
Peter Green (vocal, guitar), Jeremy Spencer (vocal, guitar, piano), John McVie (bass), Mick Fleetwood (drums). Additional musicians: Christine Perfect (piano), Duster Bennett (harmonica), Steve Gregory, Dave Howard (alto saxophones), Johnny Almond, Roland Vaughn (tenor saxophones).

Within a mere six months, Fleetwood Mac had (on record) replaced their self-conscious stance as dedicated bluesicians with an attitude which, with few exceptions, indicated that they were now playing for laughs.

Fleetwood Mac had never taken themselves that seriously on stage. Their legendary vulgarity had reached such extremes as to get them barred from London's most prestigious rock venue, the Marquee. Club manager John Gee was not amused when Fleetwood and Spencer stepped before a packed audience decorated with surgical appliances and rubber goods filled with beer.

Moreover, other managements around Britain complained vigorously about Mac's ragamuffin appearance and colorful language. Said Green, "A lot of people don't want to know us because we're so ragged and use bad language on stage." He continued defiantly, "If I want to say fuck then I will, because if I say it normally in my speech then I'm going to say it on stage too—until I get arrested for it."

He wasn't.

Efforts by The Mac to transfer their ribald sense of humor on to an album cover were immediately thwarted by Blue Horizon's British distributor CBS; the band's original title for this album was "A Good Length!" Whether or not they were influenced by the controversy then surrounding Decca and London Records' point-blank refusal to release the Rolling Stones' "Beggars Banquet," with its "offensive" graffitied lavatory wall sleeve, CBS was morally affronted by both the title and the artwork for Mac's second album. They obviously believed that the title's connotations referred to more than the drummer's height and the album's playing time. The artwork (see illustration) affirmed their misgivings.

Nevertheless, the substitute artwork—a zomboid and emaciated Fleetwood, naked save for some modest foliage—wasn't about to win any Anita Bryant Good Taste Award.

Neither, for that matter, was the music.

Like its predecessor, "Mr. Wonderful" was recorded in approximately four days. Unfortunately, this time it showed. Gone is the exuberance and spontaneity that sparked their debut. This time round, the performance is frequently slipshod, painfully repetitive and only gels (and then only just) when Green grabs the helm.

Far too often, the McVie-Fleetwood rhythm section slugged away as if marking time until the pubs opened.

Though the line-up had been increased by a four-piece sax section, the piano of Christine Perfect (soon to become Mrs. McVie) and the late Duster Bennett's harmonica, Mac—especially Jeremy Spencer—deemed it unnecessary to devote any time to rehearsal before running the tapes. "Just blow," Spencer would instruct the visitors, accepting good notes along with the bad. All very ethnic—but far too often, on the not-so-"Mr. Wonderful," this desire for authenticity (as opposed to a modicum of technical expertise) degenerates into the realms of self-parody.

Here, Jeremy Spencer must take the rap. His ongoing love affair with All Things Elmore James had become painfully embarrassing. Here he persists in playing the selfsame Dust-My-Broom-Slide-Licks on four tracks, plumbing the depths for Buster Brown's R & B jumpband opus "Dr. Brown" (itself a rework of Brown's 1959 hit "Fanny Mae") which is virtually extinguished by Spencer's James excesses.

Nobody in the band plays with effort—including Green—save for the final cut "Trying So Hard To Forget," a slow introspective blues for guitar and harp where, for once, the musicians (Green and Bennett) sound committed.

Ensnared by the limitations of the blues as Mac interpreted them, "Mr. Wonderful" gives absolutely no indication that Peter Green was

Jeremy Spencer, Peter Green, Mick Fleetwood, and John McVie with some of their younger fans.

Below: *Danny Kirwan joined Mac in 1968 at the age of nineteen. His first record with them was "Albatross."* Bottom right: *John McVie.* Opposite page: (left to right) *Jeremy Spencer, Mick Fleetwood, and Peter Green.*

about to reel off four singles which establish him as one of the more enduring of the late '60s rock composers.

Despite its manifold shortcomings, Fleetwood Mac's grass-roots momentum at the time pushed the album into the British bestseller lists, where their first album was still entrenched.

FLEETWOOD MAC

(A) **Albatross** (Green) instrumental/ (B) **Jigsaw Puzzle Blues** (Kirwan) instrumental

Produced: Mike Vernon.
(US) Epic 5-10436. Released: January 1, 1969.
(UK) Blue Horizon 3145. Released: November 22, 1968.

With one clean sweep, "Albatross" elevated Fleetwood Mac from under to overground status. Their first step away from the blues, this instrumental had the kind of crossover appeal that, in 1959, had made Santo & Johnny's "Sleep Walk" an international hit, a number with which "Albatross" is constantly compared.

Green admits to having written part of the melody in an airplane, and it shows. The only characteristic it has in common with previous Green compositions is its all-embracing sense of restraint, though in this specific case Green's layered guitars are devoid of the tension that marks his blues work. "Albatross" seems to float in suspended animation. The ethereal atmosphere is becalmed, the only movement is the gentle flicker of guitars and Fleetwood's distant and muffled tomtoms.

"Albatross" topped the British charts in December 1968, much to the chagrin of less tolerant blues purists who'd championed The Big Mac from their inception, miffed as they were at having to share *their* band with rank and file record buyers.

Fleetwood Mac didn't give a toss about accusations of "selling out." With uncanny foresight Green said at the time, "'Albatross' is my baby. It will be around when I'm dead."

(Re-released in June 1973, "Albatross" once again reached the No. 2 slot on the UK charts.)

The B-side, "Jigsaw Puzzle Blues," marks the recording debut of Mac's newest member, 19-year-old guitarist and composer Danny Kirwan. Green's protégé, Kirwan had caught the former's attention fronting Boilerhouse, a South London blues trio who had supported Fleetwood Mac at the Blue Horizon Club. So

impressed was Green with this shy young man's artistry that he solicited some dates for Boilerhouse at the Marquee and suggested they turn pro. Kirwan was keen, but the other members of Boilerhouse—Trevor Stevens (bass) and David Terry (drums)—had cold feet. That being the case, Green set about trying to build a new group around Kirwan. Unfortunately, those musicians who auditioned were not up to scratch, and in a magnanimous gesture, Green invited Kirwan into the fold.

Though Kirwan has denied having been exposed to the gypsy jazz guitarist Django Reinhardt, Mac's "Jigsaw Puzzle Blues" is identical in terms of melody and arrangement to the style of Reinhardt's celebrated group, the Quintet of the Hot Club of France.

THREE LEAD GUITARS FOR FLEETWOOD MAC

FLEETWOOD MAC is now a five-piece group in the remarkable position of having THREE lead guitarists! The new-look group made its debut at Battersea Blue Horizon Club last week before an audience that included many British blues celebrities. The trio of lead guitarists comprises Peter Green, Jeremy Spencer and new member Danny Kirwan. Kirwan has been playing solo for some time and, impressed by his talent, Peter Green and group manager Cliff Davis held auditions to se_____ ____ own band.

ENGLISH ROSE
FLEETWOOD MAC

Produced: Mike Vernon.
(US) Epic BN.26446. Released: January 1969.
(UK) Not released.

Stop Messin' 'Round (Green, Adams) Peter Green vocal/**Jigsaw Puzzle Blues** (Kirwan) instrumental/**Doctor Brown** (Brown) Jeremy Spencer vocal/**Something Inside Of Me** (Kirwan) Danny Kirwan vocal/**Evenin' Boogie** (Spencer) Jeremy Spencer vocal/**Love That Burns** (Green, Adams) Peter Green vocal/**Black Ma'gic Woman** (Green) Peter Green vocal/**I've Lost My Baby** (Spencer) Jeremy Spencer vocal/**One Sunny Day** (Kirwan) Danny Kirwan vocal/**Without You** (Kirwan) Danny Kirwan vocal/**Coming Home** (James) Jeremy Spencer vocal/**Albatross** (Green) instrumental

Personnel:
Peter Green (vocal, guitar), Jeremy Spencer (vocal, guitar, piano), Danny Kirwan (vocal, guitar), John McVie (bass), Mick Fleetwood (drums).

Peter Green said it himself (for American ears only): "'English Rose' is an album of knocked together tracks."

Perhaps realizing the shortcomings of their second British album, plus the fact that they were eager to expose the talents of new boy Danny Kirwan, Mac turned out this compilation of nine old cuts plus three new Kirwan originals—"Something Inside Of Me," "One Sunny Day" and "Without You." Strangely enough, the last two songs resurfaced towards the end of the year on "Then Play On," Fleetwood Mac's third album!

Left: *That's Mick Fleetwood underneath the football helmet with the elfin Jeremy Spencer looking on.*
Above: *A Fleetwood Mac recording session with Mick Fleetwood and John McVie.*

Again, the sleeve features Mick Fleetwood's sense of the absurd. This time, Fleetwood is photographed in drag overkill (it wasn't uncommon for the drummer to arrive at the studio thus attired), apparently as "a tribute" to a barmaid he knew.

"I get a schoolboy pleasure from shocking people," Fleetwood confessed. "I collect erotic jewelry, other erotica and those Victorian dolls that were made to be beautiful but are frightening to adults."

Fleetwood may have only been in John Mayall's army for four weeks but he sure picked up some strange habits from the old roué.

FLEETWOOD MAC

(A) Man Of The World (Green) Peter Green vocal

EARL VINCE & THE VALIANTS

(B) Somebody's Gonna Get Their Head Kicked In Tonight (Spencer) Jeremy Spencer vocal

Produced: Fleetwood Mac.
(US) Not released. (UK) Immediate IM.080. Released: April 1969.

This introspective, angst-ridden song is the first clue that all was far from well with Peter Green. His fame had left him spiritually unfulfilled and devoid of illusions about the rock'n'roll lifestyle, and this record was an open letter to that effect.

He sings:
"I guess I've got everything I need / And there's no one I'd rather be
I just wish I'd never been born / And how I wish I was in love."

Recorded in New York by Mike Vernon (ignore production credit on label), like "Albatross" and the subsequent two Fleetwood Mac Reprise singles, "Man Of The World" is dominated by Green to the extent that it could safely be considered a solo vehicle.

Though a million licks removed from Chicago's South Side, Green insisted "Man Of The World" was a blues.

"People won't think it is," said the composer, "simply because they won't have heard a blues in that sequence before. With this record, we're just trying to broaden our scope."

As a guitarist, Green stretches his fertile imagination but not the listener's patience, incorporating several facets of his fretboard technique to create a kaleidoscopic effect.

One moment it's the sighing Hawaiian guitar caw of "Albatross," the next it's pithy blueswailing, itself gently washed away yet again with more poignant atmospherics.

Green's self-pity never once degenerates into the kind of mawkish sentimentality so often the artistic downfall of lesser talents.

Truly, an exquisite record: yet this didn't deter the group's more fanatical supporters

Top left: *John McVie.* Above: *Jeremy Spencer was as well known for his vocals as was Peter Green.*

Above: *Green trades licks with B.B. King.* Opposite page: *Dame Fortune smiled, as Mac left Immediate for Reprise.*

from hollering out "Mac have gone commercial!" when, the same month, Fleetwood Mac realized an ambition and co-starred with B. B. King at London's Royal Albert Hall.

Such audience churlishness wasn't the only problem the band had to contend with. Within a year of signing to Blue Horizon (the group having given the label its commercial identity), Fleetwood Mac's recording contract was up for auction.

What followed was initially intended as a long-term arrangement between the group and Andrew Loog Oldham's self-consciously hip Immediate label; it disintegrated less than four months after this label debut was set.

The fact that "Man Of The World" quickly made the No. 2 slot on the British charts greatly increased Fleetwood Mac's stock within the music industry. John Lennon publicly declared an interest in adding Fleetwood Mac to the Beatles' year-old Apple label.

The group also received attractive tenders from CBS and Philips, but finally signed with Warner-Reprise, the label for whom Fleetwood Mac still record.

As his fixation with the Elmore James legend had indicated, Jeremy Spencer's talent was, for all his genuine enthusiasm, interpretive and not innovative.

One of the highlights of many Fleetwood Mac gigs was the sight of a gold-lamé suited and outrageously quiffed Spencer belting full tilt through a medley of Elvis Presley and other rock'n'roll hits with tongue affectionately planted in angelic cheek.

In the guise of Earl Vince & The Valiants, Fleetwood Mac, with Spencer in the spotlight, bowed to requests and devoted the B-side to an immaculate rock'n'roll parody of grease-ball mayhem, "Somebody's Gonna Get Their Head Kicked In Tonight."

So convincing was the performance that many refused to believe Earl Vince & The Valiants were those old blues blowers, Fleetwood Mac. The record is still a firm favorite with British Teddy Boys.

From now on, Fleetwood Mac's links with the blues would grow increasingly more tenuous.

FLEETWOOD MAC

(A) **Need Your Love So Bad** (John) Peter Green vocal/(B) **No Place To Go** (Burnett) Peter Green vocal

Produced: Mike Vernon.
(US) Epic S-10386. Released: August 1968.
(UK) Blue Horizon 3157. Released: July 11, 1969.

This was the only record in the Blue Horizon catalogue remotely similar in mood to "Man Of The World." As Mac were between labels and therefore hadn't scheduled an *official* follow-up, CBS with this reissue, was out to pick up sales from the more naive Fleetwood Mac fan looking for a "new" single!

THE PIOUS BIRD
OF GOOD FORTUNE
FLEETWOOD MAC

Produced: Mike Vernon.
(US) Not released. (UK) Blue Horizon 63215.
Released: August 15, 1969.

Need Your Love So Bad (John)/**Coming Home** (James)/**Rambling Pony** (Green)/***The Big Boat** (Boyd)/**I Believe My Time Ain't Long** (Spencer)/

MAC WALKS OUT ON IMMEDIATE!
Apple Records now favourites to sign Mac

FLEETWOOD MAC has walked out on Immediate — the company for which it recorded its last single, and with which it had been expected to sign a long-term deal. Manager Clifford Davis told the NME: " There have been many problems during the past four months and we have accordingly decided not to sign with Immediate." The group is currently negotiating with several other companies, including CBS and Ph... Although Apple is the leading contender to secure Mac's disc services. Davis has also been involved in ...atles' business manager Allen Klein, though he admits that he has not discarded the idea ...label as an outlet for future Mac recordings.

Davis revealed: " The Beatles have heard the new album and have been very friendly with us lately. We may sign with Apple if we can get a reasonable deal, but we are an independent team—we write, produce and record — so we may conceivably form our own label." He added that the group has secured its own publishing rights from Immediate, thus making a complete split.

Mac's next album is titled " Then Play On", and not " Bread And Kunny " as originally planned. It is due for release in September. The new outlet is ...led ... 14 tracks are a ...group — altho...

Mac Apple song deal?
JOHN LENNON IS 'INTERESTED'

THE songwriting talents of Fleetwood Mac may be signed to the Beatles' Apple music publishing offshoot if negotiations can be finalised. John Lennon said this week that he would be " interested " in having them join the company. However, the deal would be on a composing basis only — Fleetwood Mac have virtually completed plans to sign a contract with Immediate for distribution...

The Sun Is Shining (James)/**Albatross** (Green)/**Black Magic Woman** (Green)/***Just The Blues** (Boyd)/**Jigsaw Puzzle Blues** (Kirwan)/**Looking For Somebody** (Green)/**Stop Messin' 'Round** (Green, Adams)

*features Eddie Boyd (vocal, piano)

A heavily disguised compilation album, "Pious Bird Of Good Omen" can only be construed as a marketing maneuver to mislead buyers who'd been attracted to Mac via their single "Albatross," that this was Mac's eagerly awaited third album.

Even the sleeve, a photograph of a scornful and somewhat pregnant nun holding an albatross, is intended to dupe the unwitting record buyer. After all, Fleetwood Mac were notorious for their outrage.

Above: *Fleetwood Mac in transit.* Opposite page: *Jeremy Spencer claimed that Peter Green had dropped acid during their second American tour. And that was perhaps the beginning of Peter's decline.*

THEN PLAY ON
FLEETWOOD MAC

Produced: Fleetwood Mac.
(US) Reprise RS.6368. Released: October 1969.
(UK) Reprise K.44103. Released: September 1969.

Coming Your Way (Kirwan) Danny Kirwan vocal/ **Closing My Eyes** (Green) Peter Green vocal/ **Fighting For Madge** (Fleetwood) instrumental/ **When You Say** (Kirwan) Danny Kirwan vocal/ **Show-biz Blues** (Green) Peter Green vocal/**Under Way** (Green) instrumental/**One Sunny Day** (Kirwan) Danny Kirwan vocal/**Although The Sun Is Shining** (Kirwan) Danny Kirwan vocal/**Rattlesnake Shake** (Green) Peter Green vocal/**Without You** (Kirwan) Danny Kirwan vocal/**Searching For Madge** (McVie) instrumental/**My Dream** (Kirwan) Danny Kirwan vocal/**Like Crying** (Kirwan) Danny Kirwan vocal/**Before The Beginning** (Green) Peter Green vocal

Personnel:
Peter Green (vocal, guitar), **Danny Kirwan** (vocal, guitar), **John McVie** (bass), **Mick Fleetwood** (drums).

For any rock artist whose success has commenced with a debut album, it's not the second but the third LP that's more crucial. After all, unless all inspiration fails or the artist has just struck lucky, the second effort should follow in the slipstream of its progenitor.

"Then Play On" was Fleetwood Mac's third album. There couldn't have been a worse time for the cracks to begin to show. It's not that it's a bad album, or bereft of inspiration—just that it's entirely fragmented.

On the positive side, as the last two singles indicated, Fleetwood Mac had cast off their blues straitjacket and were now making music that was original and imaginative.

Though Mac's crossover acceptance was due entirely to Green's writing, something was beginning to play havoc with Green's Muse. According to Spencer, Green had experimented with hallucinogenics by this time: "Peter dropped acid on our second American tour." As to whether it altered Green's personality, Spencer replied in the affirmative, "...and there were all these girls he was mixed up with."

Even to the observer, it looked as though Green was losing his nerve and perspective, perhaps the all too familiar symptoms of post-acid ego conflict. What else was one to make of such statements as "Danny and Jeremy do much more writing than I do. I just write the odd song here and there."

True, Green had casually instructed Kirwan that on joining Fleetwood Mac, the new boy had half the next album to write (i.e. "Then Play On"), but Spencer doesn't even contribute a single song. In fact, he's not even on the album.

Confessed the Small One, "I had no inspiration...couldn't think of anything new. I was just doing Elmore James and I just couldn't think of anything else. There was nothing for me to really sing about anymore."

Spencer hadn't been put on permanent hold. Originally, "Then Play On" was to have included a bonus EP of Spencer's rock'n'roll satire as first evinced on the flip of Mac's last single, "Man Of The

Top: *Mick Fleetwood pauses for a break.* Above: *Peter Green and Jeremy Spencer. Within the next two years, both Peter and Jeremy would quit Mac.*

World." Producer Mike Vernon devoted considerable studio time to crafting this EP which, after much publicity, never materialized.

With the exception of two fiery extracts from an impromptu three hour studio jam ("Fighting For Madge" and "Searching For Madge," named after a Darlington Fleetwood Mac fan), Green and Kirwan had "Then Play On" to themselves, contributing five and seven songs respectively; one of Green's credits "Under Way" is no more than a "Son Of Albatross" doodle extracted from the above-mentioned three-hour jam.

Not only are Fleetwood Mac playing with less than their full complement of musicians, but at times they give the distinct impression that they're not working as a cohesive unit; on four cuts even Mick Fleetwood's trusty drums are dropped from the proceedings.

"People," said Green, "should know by now that they can expect anything from us." The rampant eclecticism of "Then Play On" affirms this.

Green's predominantly introspective material encompasses both his blues roots (though he'd all but ditched traditional blues imagery) and his more recent flair for melody.

"Show-biz Blues," a gritty, uptempo country blues for slide guitar and tambourine, picks up the theme of "Man Of The World"— Green's growing disenchantment with the star syndrome—and expresses his determination to Walk Closer With God. He sings:

"If I needed anybody I would take you home with me/I don't need anybody but Him and me."

His love for the Lord gets another shot on the sombre "Closing My Eyes." However, Green's preoccupation is more secular on the steamy, rollicking "Rattlesnake Shake," a masturbation manifesto.

Kirwan proves to be a far more accomplished guitarist than he is vocalist, and a better tunesmith than lyricist. That he could stand toe-to-toe with the formidable Green and get locked into a guitar duel without conceding an inch is confirmed on the album's opener "Coming Your Way."

Elsewhere, Kirwan forsakes his blues chops for a more whimsical approach. Witness "When You Say," a frail, overrepetitive pop song, later covered by John McVie's wife Christine Perfect. Another facet of young Kirwan's diverse talent was his affection for reinterpreting the highly distinctive tremolo guitar style of The Shadows' Hank B. Marvin. "My Dream" adheres to the more mellow side of The Shadows with its haunting soft focus.

As far as Fleetwood Mac were concerned, nothing, not even the blues, was sacred. Yet even in their most humorous moments, they could still deliver a killer punch. Acid blues rock and incessant quicksilver boogies were the stock in trade for guitar-laden blues bands, but on "Fighting For Madge" and "Searching For Madge," the latter made up of five snippets of tape, Mac, between psychedelic intrusions and guffaws, nail the style firmly to the wall.

Spencer probably wasn't doing the album justice when he said, from the sidelines, "'Then Play On' wasn't complete. It lacked humor." But he had a point. Nine years on, it remains as enigmatic as the day it was released. It failed to repeat the success of their previous blues trip.

Its original title was "Bread & Kunny" and it appeared dressed in two different sleeves.

FLEETWOOD MAC

(A) Oh Well Part I (Green) Peter Green vocal/**(B)
Oh Well Part 2** (Green) instrumental

Produced: Fleetwood Mac.
(US) Reprise REP.0883. Released: November
19,1969. (UK) Reprise RS.27000. Released:
September 26, 1969.

In June 1969, Green had talked of the band
releasing Danny Kirwan's inconsequential
"When You Say" as the follow-up to "Man Of
The World," yet another indication of Peter's
desire to relinquish the responsibility of
fronting Mac.

Three months later, Green had changed his
mind, and decided even in the face of oppo-
sition from his colleagues to go with his most
ambitious composition yet, "Oh Well."

He said, "I wrote it as a stage number and
then decided to try and record it. Then I
thought it would make a good single and they
made me have second thoughts."

Green's misgivings quickly vanished to the
extent that he said he was prepared to go
ahead with "Oh Well," even if it meant releasing it as his first solo venture.

Oh Ye Of So Little Faith—namely Fleetwood
and McVie, who had a five-pound wager with
Green that "Oh Well" wouldn't chart. They
didn't collect. Within two weeks of release it
was on the bestsellers' with a bullet, finally
lodging at No. 2.

"Oh Well" comes in two diametrically-
opposed parts. The first section is a frenzied
multilayered stop-start power rush replete
with immaculately dovetailed, ascending
guitar riffs.

In the opening eight bars, an abrasive
acoustic guitar firmly establishes both tempo
and rhythm pattern. The same eight bars are
then repeated, this time backed by electric
guitars and maracas. By the time the sledge-
hammer bass and tribal percussion have
been added, instrumentally "Oh Well" has
built up into an explosive chain reaction of
some of the most uninhibited flashes of primal
rock ever captured on tape. Lyrically, "Oh
Well" is confined to just two brief verses which
act as buffers to 16 bars of screaming guitars
locked in an aerial dogfight.

Though Green's self-effacing lyrics verge
on the paranoid, he seems resigned to the
point of defiance—perhaps drawing strength
from The Big G.

It was common knowledge that during
Mac's second US tour, Green had subjugated
much of his Jewishness and become fasci-

Top left: *Danny Kirwan, John McVie, Mick
Fleetwood, and Peter Green.* Top: *John McVie
and friend.* Above: *Danny Kirwan and Peter
Green exchange guitar riffs as John McVie looks
on.*

André Previn. The project was nixed due to estimated high costs.

"Oh Well Part 2" demonstrates that Green was capable of achieving such an ambitious venture using just guitar augmented with recorder, piano, cello and percussion.

Mournful in mood and biblical in inspiration (Green was running around berobed like an extra from a Cecil B. De Mille epic), "Oh Well Part 2" reveals for the first and only time Green's ability to write in the *cante hondo* (deep song) style of contemporary Spanish composer Joaquin Rodrigo.

If this wasn't enough to make the "thinking rock fan" reach for a Gideon Bible there were even more grandiose ideas flying around the Mac household. It was no big secret that both Green and Spencer were contemplating their very own religioso *Meisterwerk*.

The plan never materialized.

The success of "Oh Well" coupled with that of their two previous singles ("Albatross" and "Man Of The World") was sufficient to ensure Fleetwood Mac's *official* position as the Number One chart group in Britain throughout 1969.

nated with Buddhism and Christianity, among other things.

He admitted, "I spent a lot of time finding out about God and coming back in a big circle where I found the only thing a person could do was good. I had strong feelings that I was walking and talking with God. I was drawing away from music into just being a Christian person and it made me very happy, but it only lasted two or three weeks. Although my faith was strong it was jarred by people who didn't want to know and I made the mistake of trying to explain it to them. From now on," he concluded, "I'm going to stop going to clubs and seeing girls as much as I did because that is a waste of time."

During the recording of "Then Play On," Green also expressed a desire to record a self-penned neoclassical opus with The London Symphony Orchestra under the baton of

Above: *Live Mac: a portion of Kirwan, McVie, Spencer, Green, and Fleetwood.* Bottom: *Christine Perfect and the Melody Maker award.*

CHRISTINE PERFECT

(A) *When You Say (Kirwan)/**(B) **No Road Is The Right Road** (Perfect)

Produced: *Danny Kirwan. **Mike Vernon and Christine Perfect.
(US) Not released. (UK) Blue Horizon 57-3165.
Released: October 17, 1969.

Winning *Melody Maker's* Best British Female Vocalist Award (two years running) does not a hit single make.

BLUES JAM AT CHESS
(also titled: BLUES JAM IN CHICAGO
and FLEETWOOD MAC IN CHICAGO)

Produced: Mike Vernon and Marshall Chess.
(US) BLUES JAM IN CHICAGO Vol. 1. Blue
Horizon BH.4803. Released: 1969. BLUES JAM
IN CHICAGO Vol. 2. Blue Horizon BH.4805.
Released: 1969. FLEETWOOD MAC IN
CHICAGO Blue Horizon BH.3801. Released:
1970. Sire 2XS.6009. Released: September 16,
1977. (UK) BLUES JAM AT CHESS Blue
Horizon 7-66227. Released: December 5,
1969.

Watch Out[1] (Green) Peter Green vocal/Ooh
Baby[2] (Burnett) Peter Green vocal/South Indiana
—take 1[3] (Horton) instrumental/South Indiana—
take 2[3] (Horton) instrumental/Last Night[4] (Jacobs)
Peter Green vocal/Red Hot Jam[5] (Green) instru-
mental/I'm Worried[6] (James) Jeremy Spencer
vocal/I Held My Baby Last Night[6] (James)
Jeremy Spencer vocal/Madison Blues[6] (James)
Jeremy Spencer vocal/I Can't Hold Out[6] (James)
Jeremy Spencer vocal/I Need Your Love[7] (Hor-
ton) Walter "Shakey" Horton vocal/I Got The
Blues[7] (Horton) Walter "Shakey" Horton vocal/
World's In A Tangle[8] (Lane) Danny Kirwan
vocal/Talk With You[9] (Kirwan) Danny Kirwan
vocal/Like It This Way[9] (Kirwan) Danny Kirwan
vocal/Someday Soon Baby[10] (Spann) Otis Spann
vocal/Hungry Country Girl[10] (Spann) Otis
Spann vocal/Black Jack Blues[11] (Brown) J. T.
Brown vocal/Everyday I Have The Blues[12]
(Chatman) Jeremy Spencer vocal/Rockin'
Boogie[12] (Spencer) instrumental/Sugar Mama[13]
(Burnett) Peter Green vocal/Homework[13] (Per-
kins, Clark) Peter Green vocal

Personnel:
[1]Peter Green (vocal, guitar), Danny Kirwan
(guitar), John McVie (bass), Mick Fleetwood
(drums).
[2]Peter Green (vocal, guitar), John McVie (bass),

When Fleetwood Mac arrived in Chicago for their "Blues Jam at Chess," they rounded up all the local bluesmen to join in the recording session. Pictured: Danny Kirwan and Peter Green.

Danny Kirwan, Peter Green, and John McVie jamming it up at a recording session.

Mick Fleetwood (drums).
[3]Walter "Shakey" Horton (harmonica), Peter Green (guitar), Danny Kirwan (guitar), John McVie (bass), Mick Fleetwood (drums).
[4]Peter Green (vocal, guitar), Walter "Shakey" Horton (harmonica), Danny Kirwan (guitar), John McVie (bass), Mick Fleetwood (drums).
[5]Peter Green (guitar), Walter "Shakey" Horton (harmonica), Guitar Buddy (guitar), Honey Boy Edwards (guitar), Willie Dixon (string bass), Mick Fleetwood (drums).
[6]Jeremy Spencer (vocal, slide guitar), J. T. Brown (tenor sax), Danny Kirwan (guitar), Willie Dixon (string bass), Mick Fleetwood (drums).
[7]Walter "Shakey" Horton (vocal, harmonica), Peter Green (guitar), Danny Kirwan (guitar), Otis Spann (piano), John McVie (bass), S. P. Leary (drums).
[8]Danny Kirwan (vocal, guitar), Peter Green (guitar), Otis Spann (piano), John McVie (bass), S. P. Leary (drums).
[9]Danny Kirwan (vocal, guitar), Peter Green (guitar), Otis Spann (piano), John McVie (bass), Mick Fleetwood (drums).
[10]Otis Spann (vocal, piano), Peter Green (guitar), Danny Kirwan (guitar), John McVie (bass), Mick Fleetwood (drums).
[11]J. T. Brown (vocal, tenor sax), Jeremy Spencer (guitar), Honey Boy Edwards (guitar), Willie Dixon (string bass), Mick Fleetwood (drums).
[12]Jeremy Spencer (vocal, slide guitar), J. T. Brown (tenor sax), Peter Green (guitar), Honey Boy Edwards (guitar), Willie Dixon (string bass), Mick Fleetwood (drums).
[13]Peter Green (vocal, guitar), Danny Kirwan (guitar), Otis Spann (piano), John McVie (bass), Mick Fleetwood (drums).

In 1964, The Rolling Stones made a much-publicized pilgrimage to Chicago to record at the hallowed Chess Studios. The Stones were content to have Willie Dixon and Muddy Waters help carry in their equipment and Chuck Berry hang out in the control booth, but when, five years later, Fleetwood Mac made the same journey, they were after much more than a Chess Studio credit on their album sleeve.

At Mac's request, Willie Dixon and Chess head honcho Marshall Chess rounded up every available local bluesman, stacked the studio up with booze and set the tapes rolling. In just two days, four sides of spontaneous stomping blues combustion were in the can.

"Blues Jam At Chess"—false starts and all—is a revealing aural documentary of those January sessions.

The 22 tracks of original and traditional material comprise innumerable permutations of Mac either augmented or substituted with Willie Dixon (bass), Walter "Shakey" Horton (harmonica), Honey Boy Edwards and Guitar Buddy (guitars), J. T. Brown (tenor sax), Otis Spann (piano) and S. P. Leary (drums).

Their last blues album, "Blues Jam At Chess," avoids all the pitfalls one might expect from such an expedition. It is neither over-reverent nor self-indulgent and only occasionally sloppy. Neither do Fleetwood Mac come off second best to the Home Team.

Even four consecutive cuts of Jeremy Spencer playing Elmore James, with James' right-hand man, tenor saxist J.T. Brown, aren't too much to bear.

A posthumous Blue Horizon offering (released almost a year after the event), "Blues Jam At Chess" was at the time unfairly overlooked in the light of Mac's trilogy of hit singles which had little to do with Blues Power.

Only too aware of this, Green said petulant-

Top: *Danny Kirwan.* Above: *John McVie. John and Danny were backed up by guitarists Honey Boy Edwards and Guitar Buddy on the "Blues Jam at Chess" album.*

On sale, Friday, week ending January 18, 1969 — NEW MUSICAL EXPRESS

LIFE-LINES of FLEETWOOD MAC

	PETER GREEN	DANNY KIRWAN	JOHN McVIE	MICK FLEETWOOD	JEREMY SPENCER
Birthdate:	October 29, 1946	May 13, 1950	November 26, 1945	June 24, 1947	July 4, 1948
Personal points:	5ft. 8in., 9st. 7lb., brown eyes, brown hair	5ft. 10in., 9st. 12lb., green eyes, fair hair	5ft. 9in., 10st. 7lb., green eyes, brown hair	6ft. 6in., 10st. 4lb., hazel eyes, fair hair	5ft. 4in., 7st. 7lb., green eyes, dark brown hair
Brothers and sisters:	Linda, Leonard, Michael	—	—	—	—
Wife's name:	—	—	Christine Perfect of Chicken Shack	—	Fiona
Children:	—	—	None yet	—	Jeremy
Present home:	New Malden, Surrey	Brixton		Ealing	Paddington
Instruments played:	Guitar, harmonica	Guitar	Bass guitar	Drums	Guitar, piano
Age entered show business:	18	14	16	15	15
First professional appearance:	At 18 with Peter Barden's Shotgun Express	At 18 with Fleetwood Mac	With John Mayall	With Cheynes	1967 with Fleetwood Mac
Biggest break in career:	Forming F. Mac	Joining F. Mac	Joining F. Mac	Joining F. Mac	Joining F. Mac
Biggest disappointment:	"Need Your Love So Bad" not making it in England	None yet	—	Being sacked from John Mayall's Bluesbreakers	That "I Believe My Time Ain't Long" was not a hit
TV debut:	"Colour Me Pop"	"Dee Time"	"Colour Me Pop"	"Colour Me Pop"	"Colour Me Pop"
First important public appearance:	Windsor Jazz Festival	"Dee Time"	Windsor Jazz Festival	Windsor Jazz Festival	Windsor Jazz Festival
Hobbies:	Collect old records, antique guns, knives, etc.	Composing, playing guitar	New orange Marcos G.T., drinking	Alvis cars, collecting odd / weird knick knacks	Smoking my pipe, home record making
Biggest influence on career:	—	Listened to pop till heard John Mayall and Eric Clapton	John Mayall	—	Elmore James
Favourite colour:	Muted	Green	Brown	Claret red	Dark blue
Favourite food:	Vegetarian	Melon, steak	Anything good	Roast Duck	Egg and chips, curries, spaghetti
Favourite drink:	Fruit juice	Coke	Scotch	Wine	Orange squash, coke
Favourite clothes:	Anything comfortable	Comfortable	Casual, leather	Good, very modern suits	Denims; duffle coat, brown sweater
Favourite singers:	Little Richard, Otis Rush, B. B. King, Elvis Presley, Robert Johnson	Peter Green	Eddie Taylor, Howlin' Wolf, Leadbelly	Reg Presley, Mick Jagger	Elmore James, Tim Hardin, Cliff Richard, Little Richard, Elvis Presley
Favourite actor/actress:	Paul Newman, Hell's Angels	Ursula Andress, Humphrey Bogart	Paul Newman, Steve McQueen, Robert Wagner, Kim Novak	Lee Marvin, Hell's Angels, Brigitte Bardot	Marlon Brando
Favourite bands/instrumentalists:	Fleetwood Mac, Duster Bennett, B. B. King	Old big bands; Django Reinhardt	Duster Bennett, B. B. King, Chambers Bros.	F. Mac, Rolling Stones, Troggs	Elmore James, Otis Rush, Robert Johnson, Homesick James
Favourite composers:	Beatles, B. B. King, Duster Bennett, Danny Kirwan	Peter Green, Jeremy Spencer, Burt Bacharach, Hal David	B. B. King, Ed Sanders, Howlin' Wolf, Peter Green	Reg Presley, Jagger/ Richard, Peter Green, Beatles	Elmore James, Beatles, Peter Green
Favourite groups:	Duster Bennet, Beatles, Janis Joplin		Janis Joplin	—	Tremeloes, Electric Squitters
Car:	Red MGA		Marcos GT	Alvis, Austin 7, Bristol	—
Miscellaneous dislikes:	Insincerity	Lack of common sense	Noise, loss of temper, drunks	Pomposity, conceit	Shaving, violence
Miscellaneous likes:	Miscellaneous girls, Duster Bennett's LP "Sailin' Like I'm Happy"	Unattached women	Cowboys, Christine Perfect	Ring of a glass eye mounted on silver, de luxe sports cars, antique furniture	Reading the New Testament
Best friend:	Parrot and Mike Clifford	Peter Green	Christine Perfect, John McVie	Peter Green, Jenny Boyd	My wife Fiona
Most thrilling experience:	Going to U.S. for first time	Joining F. Mac	Christine Perfect	Watching Troggs do French TV show in Paris, Nov. '68	See "Shake Your Money Maker" go to top of charts in Scandinavia
Tastes in music:	Blues, old bands, rock and roll	Blues, pop, classical, anything good	Blues, progressive American music	Good pop, classics	Blues, rock and roll, new American folk
Pets:	Parrot, hampster		Christine Perfect, John McVie	Peter Green	Son Dicken
Personal ambition:	To live in the country with lots of animals and to be able to fish and write music	For Peter Green to stop calling me "Young Eyes"!	To play progressive music	To be successful and to own a country mansion with loads of women to pamper me	To buy a big house
Professional ambition:	To carry on playing and for people to appreciate what I'm trying to do	To be appreciated musically	The continued success of F. Mac	To go on making excellent records	To make enough money to retire on

ly: "The bulk of our fans won't like it because a lot of the blues fans have dropped us, like they do, because we've been on television and had hits." He concluded, "I get a bit angry about this old release."

Maybe with the Lord on his mind, Peter Green hadn't listened to the album as closely as he should. Careful scrutiny reveals Fleetwood Mac to be in their element: relaxed, inspired, and enthusiastic. As time was to prove, this album was, regrettably, Peter Green's blues postscript.

JEREMY SPENCER
JEREMY SPENCER

Produced: Jeremy Spencer.
(US) Not released. (UK) Reprise K.44105.
Released: January 23, 1970.

Linda (Spencer)/**The Shape I'm In** (Cathy, Blackwell)/**Mean Blues (Sic)** (Spencer)/**String-A-Long** (Duncan, Doyle)/**Here Comes Charlie (With His Dancing Shoes On)** (Spencer)/**Teenage Love Affair** (Spencer)/**Jenny Lee** (Spencer)/**Don't Go Please Stay** (Spencer)/**You Made A Hit** (Maynard)/**Take A Look Around Mrs. Brown (Sic)** (Spencer)/**Surfin' Girl** (Spencer)/**If I Could Swim The Mountain** (Spencer)

Personnel: Jeremy Spencer (vocal, guitars, slide guitar, piano), Danny Kirwan (guitar, backing vocals), John McVie (bass), Mick Fleetwood (drums, percussion), Stephen Gregory (saxophone), Peter Green (banjo) "String-A-Long."

Fleetwood Mac dropped the proposed bonus EP of Jeremy Spencer's rock 'n' roll satire from inclusion with "Then Play On" for fear "serious" rock fans would misconstrue Spencer's on-target humor.

Originally entitled "The World Of Jeremy Spencer" (a parody of the British Decca Records' unimaginative "The World Of..." reissue series) this album was first scheduled for a November 1969 release.

British rock bands are notorious for their boisterous sense of humor. But, whereas bands like the Beatles and Stones kept their laffs to the privacy of the studio, Fleetwood Mac devilishly flaunted them onstage and on record.

The acid test of any successful satirist (for instance, Frank Zappa) is the ability to lampoon the chosen subjects convincingly to that fine line where the uninitiated might be at a loss to differentiate between the parody and the genuine article.

A satirist must know every nuance of his/her subject.

On these 12 tracks (all but three written by Spencer), Spencer curls a lip, crooks a leg, shakes a shoulder and attacks everything from rockabilly to acned teen ballads, surfin' to psychedelia, blues to boogie, Presley to Pink Floyd.

Every track is a finely cut gem, particularly "Mean Blues," a wickedly accurate send-up (announcement and all) of the British Blues Boom bandwagoners, replete with 19-to-the dozen clichés, while "Don't Go Please Stay," featuring Spencer's familiar slide, is a brave pie in the face for Mac themselves.

Elsewhere, Spencer directs his scathing humor to the plethora of "socially aware" British acid bands on "Take A Look Around Mrs. Brown (Sic)." Fun-loving Jeremy introduces the cut with the sound of a technicolor yawn and exits chanting a Hari Krishna mantra.

"Surfin' Girl" has him Hanging Ten with the Beach Boys, while the grand finale "If I Could Swim A Mountain" salutes The King with a mushmouthed overwrought Presleyesque ballad, Spencer reducing the words to an inaudible mumble.

A minor classic, the album didn't sell. The sleeve couldn't have helped!

FLEETWOOD MAC

(A) The Green Manalishi (With The Two Pronged Crown) (Green) Peter Green vocal/**(B) World In Harmony** (Kirwan, Green) instrumental

Produced: Fleetwood Mac.
(US) Reprise REP.0925. Released: June 3, 1970. (UK) Reprise RS.27007. Released: May 15,1970.

Top: *Mac was joined by one of Jeremy Spencer's idols, Cliff Richards, for this photo.* Bottom: *Jeremy Spencer in concert.*

51

Danny Kirwan, John McVie, Peter Green, Jeremy Spencer, and Mick Fleetwood in 1969. The music world was shocked when Peter left the group in 1970.

filtered back to Britain from America (where the group was on tour) in January with the suggestion that Danny Kirwan was quitting the band on their return home. The same sources also claimed that more changes in both personnel and policy were imminent.

Green himself put an abrupt end to such speculation on Mac's arrival back in Britain, saying, "The band is closer than it has ever been."

This was substantiated by news that several Mac projects were in the pipeline—a "live" album drawn from three nights at the Boston Tea Party club; a Peter Green/Danny Kirwan guitar album; a Peter Green solo album by Christmas; plus 20 new Fleetwood Mac songs for the group's next studio album.

But Fleetwood Mac always did more than their fair share of pipe dreaming, and it was no real secret that Green was suffering something of an identity crisis.

In December 1969, he'd reiterated his belief that one of his colleagues should write the next single, and his guilt complex about making "easy" money hadn't gone unnoticed. Before appearing at London's Lyceum Ballroom in aid of a Jewish charity, he said, "I want to do it because I won't have to *touch* the money." He later spelled out his philanthropy. "The very least I can do is give away money I don't need."

The guitarist was to continue freely distributing his "unclean" wealth up until quite recently. "He must have given away tens of thousands," said Green's father in 1977. Despite an estimated annual income (from record and publishing royalties) of £30,000 Green has been known to bum his cab fare home.

It was during the second week in April 1970 that Peter Green dropped the bombshell—he was leaving Fleetwood Mac. Green was to play his last gig with the band on May 24, at London's Roundhouse.

Like the British rock public, the band was shocked. They had no option but to cancel a British tour scheduled to begin on June 1.

Rumors of dissent within the group had

Antimaterialism had become a part of the Woodstock subculture. For every band that was genuinely willing to give free concerts and financial support to *their* community (e.g. The Grateful Dead), there were dozens more who exploited this "altruism" for their own ends.

As events would prove, Green wasn't bullshitting when on leaving Fleetwood Mac he said, "There are many reasons why I'm leaving; the main thing being that I feel it is time for a change. I want to change my whole life, because I don't want to be all a part of the conditioned world and as much as possible I'm getting out of it."

As God would have it, Green was to release one more self-penned Fleetwood Mac single before fading into obscurity, "Green Manalishi."

During this stage in their recording career, Fleetwood Mac never opted for a predictable fail-safe, the-hits-keep-on-coming formula. "Green Manalishi" was as different to "Oh Well" as "Oh Well" was to "Man Of The World."

Again, it is Green who occupies the driver's seat. An aura of supernatural doom pervades, as the singer wrestles with the Devil, literal or metaphorical. Or both!

Guitars and percussion beat out a heavy foreboding riff, intercut with a persistent and menacing four-in-the-bar chord figure played to give a tape-loop effect. Stylistically, "Green Manalishi" explores the kind of controlled heavy metal dynamic tension favored by Cream.

"World In Harmony" sounds as though it could have been a dry run for the proposed Green/Kirwan guitar album.

pril 11, 1970

MAC LEADER QUITS
Peter Green leaving on May 25

The New Musical Express *headlined Green's leave-taking.*

One of Christine Perfect's first professional gigs was with the band, Shades of Blue, playing bass. She later made several recordings with Chicken Shack before forming her own group. Opposite page: Christine and her perfect mini.

CHRISTINE PERFECT

Produced: Mike Vernon and Christine Perfect; *Danny Kirwan.
(US) Sire SASD.7522. Released: September 16, 1977. (UK) Blue Horizon 7-63860. Released: June 12, 1970.

Crazy 'Bout You Baby[1] (Williamson)/I'm On My Way[1] (Malone)/Let Me Go (Leave Me Alone)[1] (Perfect)/Wait And See[1] (Perfect)/Close To Me[2] (Perfect)/I'd Rather Go Blind[3] (Jordan, Foster)/ *When You Say[4] (Kirwan)/And That's Saying A Lot[1] (Jackson, Godfrey)/No Road Is The Right Road[5] (Perfect)/For You[1] (Perfect)/I'm Too Far Gone (To Turn Around)[1] (Otis, Hendriks)/I Want You[1] (White)

Personnel:
[1]Christine Perfect (vocal, keyboards), Rick Hayward, Top Topham (guitars), Martin Dunsford (bass), Chris Harding (drums).
[2]Christine Perfect (vocal, keyboards), Rick Hayward, Top Topham (guitars), Andy Silvester (bass), Chris Harding (drums).
[3]Chicken Shack: Stan Webb (guitar), Christine Perfect (vocal, keyboards), Andy Silvester (bass), Dave Bidwell (drums).
[4]Christine Perfect (vocal, keyboards), Danny Kirwan (guitar), Rick Hayward, Top Topham (guitars), John McVie (bass), Chris Harding (drums).
[5]Christine Perfect (vocal, keyboards), plus unidentified session musicians.
"When You Say" arranged John Bennett. "No Road Is The Right Road" arranged Derek Wadsworth. "Crazy 'Bout You Baby," "I'm On My Way" arranged Terry Noonan.

The daughter of a music professor, Christine Perfect trained as a classical pianist, with the result that she loathed the piano by the time she reached her teens. At 16, Christine and a girlfriend left their Birmingham home for London, where they hoped to impress talent scouts with their rendition of Everly Brothers numbers. Disapproving parents quickly dragged their "wayward" daughters back to the bosom of the family, Christine being packed off to Art College. She graduated five years later, "a uselessly qualified sculptress."

Her college days weren't completely wasted since it was there that she fell in with the city's burgeoning R & B scene, where she met guitarist Spencer Davis.

They dated and together occasionally provided the vocal front line for the university jazz band. Soon Spencer was to team up with local 14-year-old boy wonder Stevie Winwood and make a little history. Christine, however, bided her time, joining an inauspicious local outfit, the Shades of Blue, with whom she played bass.

If you've ever visited Birmingham, you'll appreciate why, when school was finally out, Christine fled to London. Her artistic flair landed her a job dressing windows in London's West End: Regent Street, to be precise. Music was the last thing on her mind when she renewed her friendship with former Shades of Blue members Stan "The Man" Webb and Andy Silvester, who shanghaied her into joining a band they were forming for Blue Horizon Records.

Originally called Sounds Of Blue, they renamed themselves Chicken Shack (after a Jimmy Smith composition). Christine would be required to play piano and sing when the boisterous Webb needed to take a breather or a beer. After a crash course in Freddie King albums, where she checked out King's pianist Sonny Thompson, Christine was flung in at the

CHRISTINE PERFECT HAS QUIT!

CHRISTINE PERFECT has quit the music business! The girl, for whom a great future was predicted when she left Chicken Shack in 1968 to go solo, has announced that she is giving up singing altogether. Her decision coincides with the release of her new Blue Horizon album which bears her name as its title. Her withdrawal from the music scene takes immediate effect. She told the NME this week: "I shall be doing no more live dates, and making no more records."

Above: *After her marriage to John McVie, Christine left Chicken Shack to devote herself to domestic duties.*

deep end, playing five sets a night, seven nights a week for a month at Hamburg's scuzzy Star Club.

On their return to England, Chicken Shack debuted at the Annual Windsor Blues & Jazz Festival, as fate would have it, on the very same day that Fleetwood Mac introduced themselves to the British public.

Following in Fleetwood Mac's bedenimed slipstream, Shack notched up two chart albums of earnest Freddie King-obsessed blues. Webb's ribald stage antics and guitar dexterity would have made him a perfect first reserve for Fleetwood Mac, but the novelty of a blonde British girl singing and playing the blues with panache was just as responsible for giving Chicken Shack its identity. In fact, Chicken Shack's solitary hit single, a carbon copy of Etta James' classic "I'd Rather Go Blind" (later covered by Rod Stewart) was entirely Christine's show.

Ironically, "I'd Rather Go Blind" was the last Chicken Shack single to feature the dulcet tones of the woman. She quit the day it was released!*

Christine had recently married Fleetwood Mac's bassist John McVie whom she'd first encountered when both Mac and Shack co-starred at a blues night at London's Savile Theatre.

McVie proposed four months later at the Bag O'Nails Club, and they married in August

*Chicken Shack Albums:
FORTY BLUES FINGERS FRESHLY PACKED AND READY TO SERVE
(US) Epic BN.26414.   (UK) Blue Horizon 7-63203.
O.K. KEN?
(US) Blue Horizon BH.7705. (UK) Blue Horizon 7-63209.

1968. As both were extremely busy pursuing their own careers, their paths seldom crossed, and Mrs. McVie decided to call it a day with Chicken Shack and become a *hausfrau.* Such domesticity was short-lived and months later, flushed with the kudos of winning the British Female Vocalist category in *Melody Maker*'s 1969 Readers' Poll (and not deterred by the lure of Big Money), Christine hung up her apron, formed her own band, and hit the road.

The venture lasted less than six months. "My own band was just a massive weight," she admitted. "The first gigs were diabolical and promoters were naturally disappointed because we were being paid a lot of money." By the time the Christine Perfect Band had tightened up their act, it was too late—bookings were thin on the ground and debts were piling up.

Come June 1970, Christine prepared to cut her losses. Again putting marriage before music, she turned down the opportunity to promote a solo single ("When You Say") on BBC-TV's prime time "Top Of The Pops" plug show, in favor of a holiday with John in Greece. Going solo was, in her own words, "a desperate effort, a disaster—and that's putting it mildly."

And who are we to argue?

As Christine Perfect's solo album makes only too clear, it was "a rushed job." Lacking in confidence, direction, inspiration and continuity, the overall impression is of a hastily performed demo. Quite frankly, Christine Perfect's attempted elevation by her counselors from sideperson to solo star on the strength of one Top 20 single and a Readers' Award (almost invariably a shortcut to obscurity) was pushing it.

On the album, Christine seems to persist in singing in one key and one mode. Apart from the inclusion of the Chicken Shack hit, the collection's only saving grace are the two tracks which comprised her last solo single.

"When You Say," replete with Palm Court strings and the more melodious characteristics of Danny Kirwan's guitar (the Old Man plucks bass), has the edge over Mac's version. With its Stax undertones, "No Road Is The Right Road" displays an embryonic songwriting talent. One more plus: her aloof, ultracool vocalizing was refreshingly devoid of butch blues histrionics, though as yet technically unevolved.

Time, as they say, worked wonders.

Left: *Christine with Chicken Shack.* Above: *After several months of domestic life, Christine formed her own group and hit the road.*

KILN HOUSE
FLEETWOOD MAC

Produced: Fleetwood Mac.
(US) Reprise RS.6408. Released: September 18, 1970. (UK) Reprise K.54001. Released: September 18, 1970.

This Is The Rock (Spencer) Jeremy Spencer vocal/Station Man (Kirwan, Spencer, McVie) Danny Kirwan vocal/Blood On The Floor (Spencer) Jeremy Spencer vocal/Hi Ho Silver (Waller, Kirkeby) Jeremy Spencer vocal/Jewel Eyed Judy (Kirwan, Fleetwood, McVie) Danny Kirwan vocal/Buddy's Song (Holly) Jeremy Spencer vocal/Earl Grey (Kirwan) instrumental/One Together (Spencer) Jeremy Spencer vocal/Tell Me All The Things You Do (Kirwan) Danny Kirwan vocal/Mission Bell (Michael, Hodges) Jeremy Spencer vocal

Personnel:
Jeremy Spencer (vocal, guitar, piano), Danny Kirwan (vocal, guitar), John McVie (bass), Mick Fleetwood (drums).

Shortly after the release of "Kiln House," taciturn John McVie opined, "The album was a product of these confused times." Ironically, Fleetwood Mac's first post-Green waxing is far less fragmented than its predecessor "Then Play On."

On his abdication from Fleetwood Mac, Green, who according to Spencer saw the chart-topping Mac as (of all things) "a sinking ship," nominated Spencer as leader-elect.

Spencer, who, by his own volition, hadn't participated in the making of "Then Play On," harbored no illusions about his capabilities. He said, "I didn't feel I could do it. All I could play was rock 'n' roll. Peter was a developed musician. I couldn't do the stuff that people

now expected us to play. Danny could play, but didn't have Peter's stage presence."

Sure enough, Spencer's sizeable contribution to "Kiln House" (three originals, one co-credit and three "covers") was deep-rooted in '50s Americana. Unlike Spencer's side-splitting solo album, not all of these flashbacks are caricatures.

The opening "This Is The Rock," a loose-hipped rockabilly, pays tribute to the Sun Sound. "Hi Ho Silver," an R & B 12-bar of confused pedigree (credited to Fats Waller, but identical to the song of the same name immortalized by Joe Turner and Johnny Burnette), and "Buddy's Song," also play it straight. The latter is an affectionate elegy by Mrs. Ella Holly for her late son Buddy, firmly based on "Peggy Sue Got Married."

"Blood On The Floor," as the title suggests, is Spencer's satire on all those maudlin country and western dirges, and "One To-

Mick with fiancée Jenny Boyd, whom he later married. Jenny's sister Patti was married to Beatle George Harrison at the time. Opposite page: (Left) Peter Green with Fleetwood Mac. (Right) Peter made his debut as a soloist months after leaving Mac.

gether" ridicules the kind of wimpery once dished up by Ozzie and Harriet Nelson's doe-eyed son Ricky.

The originality on this album comes courtesy of the underrated Danny Kirwan, who, though lacking the driving vision of his erstwhile mentor Green, rises to the occasion with aplomb.

To this day, Fleetwood Mac still feature Kirwan's insidious and deceptively low-key "Station Man" in their stage act. Here it's duetted by Kirwan and a mixed-down Christine McVie. Undoubtedly the album's premier cut, the melody is neatly slung over the kind of dense broken riffing which has become a trademark with numerous mid-70's American West Coast bands like Little Feat.

Pivoted on a repetitious four-bar phrase, Kirwan's instrumental "Earl Grey" presents the guitarist in a more subdued mood, while "Tell Me All The Things You Do" confirms his ability to both write and perform a tight sinewy rock number.

"Jewel Eyed Judy" co-credits Kirwan alongside McVie and Fleetwood and was suggested by their manager as a single. The Mac vetoed this, and no singles were forthcoming from "Kiln House."

Prior to Green's departure, Fleetwood had declared that the band were at the zenith of their British popularity. Since they—unlike Cream and Ten Years After—had failed to show any profit from several coast-to-coast American tours, making it in the US of A, Green or no Green, was now their number-one priority.

And perhaps this record's voguish laid-back quality was why "Kiln House" was Fleetwood Mac's most successful to date with an American audience, though hardly an outright smash.

Prior to taking this album on the road (first stop New Orleans) it was agreed that the Mac sound needed fleshing out. Rather than placing an ad in the *Times*, Fleetwood Mac turned to their bassist's spouse, the "retired" Christine McVie (née Perfect), incidentally responsible for the album's artwork. She officially threw in her lot with the Mac in August.

JEREMY SPENCER

(A) Linda (Spencer)/**(B) Teenage Darling** (Spencer)

Produced: Jeremy Spencer.
(US) Not released. **(UK)** Reprise RS.27002.
Released: October 17, 1970.

A pastiche of Tommy Roe's "Sheila," itself a blatant ripoff of Buddy Holly's "Peggy Sue." Muffled drums gallop, an acoustic guitar frantically strums the clipped chords and Spencer hiccups the vocal in a thin nasal whine.

In Britain, it seems, there weren't enough girls around named Linda to put it in the charts. However, in Holland, it was quite the reverse, and it was a sizable hit.

THE END OF THE GAME
PETER GREEN

Produced: Peter Green.
(US) Not released. **(UK)** Reprise RSLP.9006.
Released: November 20, 1970.

Bottoms Up (Green)/**Timeless Time** (Green)/
Descending Scale (Green)/**Burnt Foot** (Green)/

Hidden Depth (Green)/The End Of The Game
(Green)

Personnel:
Peter Green (guitar), Zoot Money (piano), Nick
Buck (keyboards), Alex Dmochowski (bass),
Godfrey Maclean (drums, percussion).

A prophetically entitled album of directionless
instrumental acid-rock jams—only a psychedelic light show is missing—which brings into
painfully sharp focus the sudden, and seemingly irreversible, demise of Peter Green.

The music reflects Green's confusion. On
leaving Fleetwood Mac, he'd stated optimis-
tically, "I want to get one hundred percent into
music. I want to do lots of jamming with different groups and musicians."

Eight years on, "The End Of The Game"
remains his swan-song. Save for two disconso-
late singles, and single-track guest appearances on B. B. King's 1971 "London Sessions"
and Fleetwood Mac's "Penguin" two years
later, he never made another record.

The handful of unpublicized live appearances that the white-robed Green made
around this time, mainly in London pubs,
were, true to his declaration, unrehearsed and
open-ended. An exception was his advertised
gig with a one-off John Mayall Band at 1970's
star-studded Bath Festival.

Two years later, Green lost his nerve after
tentatively agreeing to fill in for the late Les
Harvey in Stone the Crows at the Lincoln Festival. He chickened out, claiming that he just
couldn't face an audience (Yes, guitarist Steve
Howe stepped in at the last moment).

Along with Pink Floyd's madcap genius, the
definitive acid casualty Syd Barrett, Peter
Green remains the most enigmatic figure in
British rock lore. The events that preceded
Green's rejection of the star syndrome have
become a miasma of fact and fantasy.

On his withdrawal from Fleetwood Mac,
Green involved himself with a German
commune. Subsequent sightings had him
working as a gravedigger, barman, as a
member of a kibbutz, employed as a hospital
orderly, and even venturing into the hotel
business.

His only contacts with the music business in
the last five years have been strictly peripher-
al—hanging out in rock clubs and making hit-
and-run appearances with a small-time
Santanaesque group called Little Free Rock
(with whom one of the authors occasionally
gigged).

Hope springs eternal that Peter Green will
one day, miraculously, pick up the threads.

Peter Green's debut

PLAYING guitar to the sole
accompaniment of either
piano or organ, Peter Green chose
a concert at Barnet on Sunday to
make his first appearance since
leaving Fleetwood Mac.

In sympathy with the teenage
organisers' creditable aims of keeping admission down to five bob for
a se...

Jeremy Spencer's dramatic disappearance rocked the music world.

FLEETWOOD MAC

(A) Dragonfly (Kirwan, Davies) Danny Kirwan, Christine McVie vocals/**(B) Purple Dancer** (Fleetwood, McVie, Kirwan) instrumental

Produced: Fleetwood Mac.
(US) Not released. (UK) Reprise RS.27010.
Released: March 5, 1971.

Christine McVie's first official Fleetwood Mac single and Jeremy Spencer's last, "Dragonfly" was a mellifluous Danny Kirwan song with shades of "Albatross" and West Coast overtones.

Justifiably, it got favorable reviews, but was totally overshadowed by yet another Mac melodrama.

About three o'clock on a late February afternoon, Jeremy Spencer walked out of his Los Angeles hotel to visit a bookstore he regularly frequented. The band was two weeks into their sixth American tour—their most successful to date—and were due to start a four-day stint at L.A.'s Whisky A Go Go.

Spencer didn't show for that evening's gig and by the end of the night the group's manager Clifford Davis contacted the Los Angeles Police Department.

Five days later, Spencer was tracked down to a religious colony, the Children of God. At the time, Spencer's behavior was likened to that of a vegetable. Davis was first to see him at the Children of God colony, and staggered out, describing the guitarist as a "star-struck child." Another eyewitness account claimed Spencer was "walking around in a daze like a zombie."

Even before Fleetwood Mac's plane touched down at L.A.'s International Airport from San Francisco, Spencer had told roommate Mick Fleetwood of his anxiety concerning the group's visit to the earthquake-ravaged L.A. Spencer went so far as to say he felt that "evil" was "out to get" him.

With his waiflike hippy appearance, the 22-year-old Spencer was ideal God-fodder for the Sacred Sales Spiel of L.A.'s most extremist Hell and Damnation Brigade. But like his erstwhile colleague Peter Green, Spencer's behavior was unpredictable. Though apparently he packed a Bible (a miniature volume sewn into his jacket) from his early days with The Mac, Spencer as a performer could plumb the depths of bad taste.

"He could be so vulgar," said Christine McVie, "it would make you wince." Yet when strangers were around he could be retiring to the point of misanthropy.

When Davis, acting on a reliable tip-off, entered the Children of God's four-story warehouse H.Q. in downtown L.A., those inside denied point-blank that Spencer was on the premises.

Davis, flanked by two Mac roadies, Keene and McDonnell, was refused entrance until he fabricated a story about Jeremy's wife Fiona being seriously ill. Even then, it wasn't until after much verbal slanging that Spencer appeared—hair shorn and dressed in "dirty" clothes.

His name had been changed, to the biblical "Jonathan."

Davis and Spencer talked for three hours, the guitarist explaining that he no longer wanted to work, that, surprise, surprise, the world was coming to an end, and that his first priority was to save his soul.

"I must admit," said Davis, "that he appeared most sensible during our long talk."

When asked what would become of his wife and two young children, Spencer replied nonchalantly, "Jesus loves. Jesus will take care of them...." During the conversation, two Godheads continually rubbed the guitarist's arms chanting "Jesus Loves You."

"He'd been brainwashed," said Keene. "It nearly killed me to see him."

Jeremy's decision to quit Fleetwood Mac wasn't as impulsive as it seemed to the rest of the band. He said, "I asked God before I left for the tour to somehow soon make a change and show me something." Two days prior to his disappearance he'd confided in a bunch of Seattle Jesus Freaks. "I'd never told anybody else that I felt that I couldn't go on any longer with the band, but I felt I could tell *them*."

Though Spencer hadn't declared his disillusionment with the Material World in song, he felt much the same way as Peter Green. "On this tour, we were going down O.K. out of respect more than anything else," Spencer revealed. "We drove to the Fillmore West in this big Rolls Royce. It was different from the first time we went there. Then the music was really heavy blues. We didn't have very much money and we weren't in the best hotels, but it was more real."

Spencer's insecurities about the group's direction had been brought nearer to the surface when, after the Fillmore show, the group returned to their hotel and listened to an old tape of the band featuring Green.

Lamented Spencer, "We listened to 'Black Magic Woman' and there were these incredible guitar leads. Then some of my things came on and I couldn't stand listening to it. I said, 'That sounds horrible. It sounds like shit!' Maybe, to some people it sounded good but

Christine plays the Wurlitzer with Mac for British television.

Jeremy Spencer and John McVie shortly before Jeremy disappeared to join the religious group, Children of God.

how could I go on with it? I just had to leave. I went to bed and said, 'God, soon. I can't go on with this any longer.'" Another post-acid crisis of confidence? Spencer took his first acid trip during Fleetwood Mac's 1968 American debut. He recalled, "It was ecstasy for the first four hours until I became conscious of leaving 'self' behind. Then it was torment."

The tour over, Spencer returned to Britain and married Fiona, a 16-year-old who had borne his child a year earlier. "She was the first person to ask about Jesus and God seriously with me." In the three years before dropping out of the band he'd helped establish, Spencer did a lot of soul-searching. "Acid trips and dope, fame and fortune," he said, "pride and conceit, idleness and every other sin took hold of me from the start of the material success of the band, like to the point where they'd never taken hold of me before; and to the point where I was reading all sorts of mystical books.

"And thinking Jesus was a mystical myth and believing everything I read. I thought I was super-spiritual and a potential Christ! There were many other mind-power trips that I am too embarrassed to discuss.

"Music was becoming secondary, I was coming first, and I didn't even seem to consider others. I was making my wife's life hell, and others around me, though I managed to entertain them sometimes by being 'funny.'"

Spencer's account of the day he left Fleetwood Mac starts with him meeting Children of God member Apollos as he was leaving the L.A. bookshop. "Apollos sang me a couple of songs. He asked me if I'd ever asked Jesus into my heart. I told him I had with some Billy Graham followers in Copenhagen about a year previous, but I didn't experience a great difference, so I thought I'd try again."

Eureka!

Several days after the warehouse incident, Spencer found "enlightenment" en route to the Children of God's Texas Clinic.

With the exception of one album (see page 72), Jeremy Spencer, like Peter Green, has never returned to his former lifestyle. Of late, the Children of God sect has attracted much notoriety from the popular press who have homed in on their allegedly licentious lifestyle, and their "Hookers For Jesus" recruitment campaign.

As for Fleetwood Mac themselves, they'd admirably weathered the storm caused by Green's sudden departure from the group and weren't about to capitulate now. Green was airlifted in to complete their American commitments.

Desperate situations call for desperate measures and for the remainder of the tour, Mac made do with a set thrown together— "Black Magic Woman," an hour's jamming, and the occasional vocal from Danny and Christine. "We'd arrive at a gig," said John McVie, "and suddenly find ourselves onstage staring at an audience without a clue what to play. We were scared stiff."

Perverse to the very end, Green saw Mac's predicament as something of a joke. "He never said much onstage," added McVie, "but occasionally Peter would amble up to the mike and say, 'Yankee bastards' and laugh!"

THE ORIGINAL FLEETWOOD MAC
FLEETWOOD MAC

Produced: Mike Vernon.
(US) Sire SR.6045. Released: November 4, 1977. (UK) CBS 63875. Released: May 14, 1971.

Drifting (Green) instrumental/**Leaving Town Blues** (Green) Peter Green vocal/**Watch Out** (Green) Peter Green vocal/**A Fool No More** (Green) Peter Green vocal/**Mean Old Fireman** (Trad arr. Spencer) Jeremy Spencer vocal/**Can't Afford To Do It** (Williamson) Jeremy Spencer vocal/**Fleetwood Mac** (Green) instrumental/**Worried Dream** (King) Peter Green vocal/**Love That Woman** (Leake)/**Allow Me One More Show** (Spencer) Jeremy Spencer vocal/**First Train Home** (Green) Peter Green vocal/**Rambling Pony No. 2** (Green) Peter Green vocal

Personnel: Peter Green (vocal, guitar, harmonica), Jeremy Spencer (vocal, guitar, piano), John McVie (bass), Mick Fleetwood (drums, washboard) plus Christine Perfect (piano).

Often referred to as "Before The Split," this album of studio out-takes comprises hitherto unreleased pre-Danny Kirwan cuts, some of which are apparently not group performances.

According to producer Mike Vernon, "Mean Old Fireman" and "Allow Me One More Show" are part of an audition that Spencer's pre-Mac band, the Levi Set, recorded for Blue Horizon. "Fleetwood Mac" itself may well be a Bluesbreakers' track, with Aynsley Dunbar and not Mick Fleetwood on drums.

A not unimpressive companion to Fleetwood Mac's very first album.

Mick Fleetwood on drums during a recording session.

PETER GREEN

(A) Heavy Heart (Green, Watson, Kelly, Chewaluza)/**(B) No Way Out** (Green, Watson)

Produced: Peter Green.
(US) Not released. (UK) Reprise RS.27012.
Released: June 11, 1971.

A meandering and uninspired flirtation with rudimentary Afro rhythms, Green's once-omniscient guitar is mixed below the percussion. Introspective and sombre, it gets nowhere slowly. Like the crudely recorded B-side, it sounds more like a half-baked run-through than an actual take.

Above: *Mac's vocal style changed after Jeremy Spencer's departure, but Danny Kirwan was on hand to take up the slack.* Right: *A shaggy-haired Mick Fleetwood with Danny Kirwan.* Opposite page: *Mac auditioned twenty-four musicians to fill Jeremy Spencer's spot in the group. In the lineup: Danny Kirwan, Jeremy Spencer, Christine McVie, John McVie, and Mick Fleetwood.*

BLACK MAGIC WOMAN
FLEETWOOD MAC

Produced: Mike Vernon.
(US) Epic EG.30632. Released: August 25, 1971. (UK) Not released.

My Heart Beat Like A Hammer (Spencer)/Merry Go Round (Green)/Long Grey Mare (Green)/Hellhound On My Trail (Trad arr. Green)/Shake Your Moneymaker (James)/Looking For Somebody (Green)/No Place To Go (Burnett)/My Baby's Good To Me (Spencer)/I Loved Another Woman (Green)/Cold Black Night (Spencer)/The World Keeps On Turning (Green)/Got To Move (Williamson)/Stop Messin' 'Round (Green, Adams)/Jigsaw Puzzle Blues (Kirwan)/Doctor Brown (Brown)/Something Inside Of Me (Kirwan)/Evenin' Boogie (Spencer)/Love That Burns (Green, Adams)/Black Magic Woman (Green)/I've Lost My Baby (Spencer)/One Sunny Day (Kirwan)/Without You (Kirwan)/Coming Home (James)/Albatross (Green)

Straight repackage of Mac's first two US albums which, as luck would have it, would capitalize on the upcoming success of "Future Games."

FUTURE GAMES
FLEETWOOD MAC

Produced: Fleetwood Mac.
(US) Reprise RS.6465. Released: November, 1971. (UK) Reprise K.44153. Released: September 3, 1971.

Woman Of 1000 Years (Kirwan) Danny Kirwan vocal/Morning Rain (McVie) Christine McVie vocal/What A Shame (Welch, Fleetwood, Kirwan, McVie, McVie) instrumental/Future Games (Welch) Bob Welch vocal/Sands Of Time (Kirwan) Danny Kirwan vocal/Sometimes (Kirwan) Danny Kirwan vocal/Lay It All Down (Welch) Bob Welch vocal/Show Me A Smile (McVie) Christine McVie vocal

Personnel:
Danny Kirwan (vocal, guitar), Bob Welch (vocal, guitar), Christine McVie (vocal, keyboards), John McVie (bass), Mick Fleetwood (drums).

The very first thing Bob Welch noticed on arrival at Fleetwood Mac's Hampshire retreat was Jeremy Spencer's gold lamé suit hanging up behind a door; gone, but not forgotten.

Bob Welch was the first of 24 musicians to audition for the group's vacant guitar slot. He found Fleetwood Mac listless and seemingly on the verge of throwing in the towel.

A native Californian, Welch expected to reel off the group's Greatest Hits. He had no idea he would have to provide his new employers with fresh material. "They didn't know what they were gonna do, they were wide open to any suggestions," he remembered.

Prior to joining Mac, Welch worked Las Vegas with The Seven Souls, a showband for incoming soul stars like James Brown and Aretha Franklin. When, in 1969, The Seven Souls broke up in Hawaii, Welch and two of

MAC'S NEW MAN

FLEETWOOD Mac manager ... placing ... with an ... Cornick ... spot, al ... will con ... propose ...

On sale Friday, week ...

this week announced the name of ... elch from ... is 25-ye ... to Britain ... 13 first music ... Welch is ...

ending April 24, 1971

the group's new member who is recently, and met Mac through Judy San Francisco, who has been playing ... dian to be auditioned for the vacant ... now rehearsing with the band, and ... outfit does no ...

The wife of Jethro Tull's bassist Glenn Cornick, Judy Wong, told Bob Welch about the opening in Mac after Spencer left.

the group moved to Paris and formed Head West. A biracial R & B trio, the group cut one album for Disque Vogue before breaking up. On the eve of taking up a job with the Memphis-based Stax label, Welch was put on to Mac by a mutual friend, Judy Wong, the wife of Jethro Tull bassist Glenn Cornick.

Spencer having followed Green in the quest for spiritual fulfillment, Fleetwood Mac were now hellbent on establishing a brand new group identity.

As "Future Games" vividly illustrates, they were starting all over again from scratch. Not once does the album give the remotest indication of their past affiliations. It's as if their two decamped guitarists had never existed.

In style, content, direction, performance and production, "Future Games" is a tasteful and thoroughly convincing reflection of bright-eyed, post-acid West Coast rock without being imitative or clichéd.

Shades of CSN & Y, Love, and the Grateful Dead's "American Beauty" period proliferate without subjugating Mac's own revitalized personality.

This album is make or break time for Fleetwood Mac. Realizing their predicament, they maximize their collective talent and win the day with a record strong on pert, up-tempo songs, memorable though not obvious melodies, relaxed yet ever so tight vocal harmonies, interweaving jangling guitar lines, the whole liberally dosed in Vitamin C.

With songs overshooting the three-minute barrier, their open-ended arrangements provide the ideal setting for disciplined bouts of jamming, and the opportunity to take a song like Bob Welch's title track and build climax upon climax.

Indeed, Welch's presence invigorates the group. "Bob has been instrumental in bringing us together as a unit," claimed Christine McVie, herself a deal more surefooted than on her last Mac outing. She added, "He's like a breath of fresh air to us because everyone was on the verge of cracking up when Jeremy left."

The clincher was taking the album to the American public. A tour was extended by two weeks, house records were smashed in Miami, San Bernardino and Baltimore, and at New York's Fillmore East, the "new look" Mac topped even the formidable Van Morrison. Chartwise, the group had finally established a firm footing.

It appeared that, after all, there was a light at the end of the tunnel. But was it an oncoming train?

FLEETWOOD MAC

(A) Sands Of Time (Kirwan) Danny Kirwan vocal/**(B) Lay It All Down** (Welch) Bob Welch vocal

**Produced: Fleetwood Mac.
(US) Reprise REP.1057. Released: November 10, 1971. (UK) Not released.**

Not the most obvious track to push as a single, "Sands Of Time" wafts in on a gentle wave of cross-current rhythms vaguely reminiscent of the lighter side of the Byrds—more jingle than jangle. Once the mundane riff has been stated and Kirwan has made one of his ever-so-tasteful guitar comments, no effort is made to develop this song further. As it doesn't benefit from a strong hook, Kirwan's frail, lackluster voice renders the melody nothing more than remotely pleasant. Once gone, soon forgotten.

FLEETWOOD MAC
GREATEST HITS
FLEETWOOD MAC

Produced: Mike Vernon and Fleetwood Mac.
(US) Not released. (UK) CBS 69011. Released:
November 1971.

The Green Manalishi (With The Two Pronged
Crown) (Green)/Oh Well Part 1 (Green)/Oh
Well Part 2 (Green)/Shake Your Moneymaker
(James)/Need Your Love So Bad (John)/Rattle
Snake Shake (Green)/Dragonfly (Kirwan,
Davies)/Black Magic Woman (Green)/Albatross
(Green)/Man Of The World (Green)/Stop Mess-
in' 'Round (Green, Adams)/Love That Burns
(Green, Adams)

The tracks speak for themselves. For those
latecomers unfamiliar with Fleetwood Mac's
original guitar triumvirate, this album is still
the ideal crash course.

NIGEL WATSON & PETER GREEN

(A) Beasts Of Burden (Watson, Green) Nigel
Watson vocal/(B) Uganda Woman (Watson) Nigel
Watson vocal

Produced: no credit.
(US) Not released. (UK) Reprise K.14141.
Released: January 21, 1972.

For his last credited appearance on record to
date, Peter Green plays second string to a
complete unknown, one Nigel Watson—a
relative of Green's manager Clifford Davis.
Tomtoms pound unmercifully, Green's guitar
strafes the doomy atmosphere while the
Watson fellow bleats portentously about man's
cruelty to his four-legged friends. The equally
dire flip sounds like a theme for a White
Hunter B-movie.

FLEETWOOD MAC

(A) The Green Manalishi (With The Two Pronged
Crown) (Green) Peter Green vocal/(B) Oh Well—
Part 1 (Green) Peter Green vocal

Produced: Fleetwood Mac.
(US) Reprise REP.1079. Released: March 15,
1972. Reprise GRE.0108. Released: March 12,
1973. (UK) Reprise K.14174. Released: March
1973.

Two hits for the price of one, issued and re-
issued as part of the label's Back To Back
oldies series.

*Fleetwood Mac before Bob Welch: Mick
Fleetwood, John McVie, Christine McVie, Jeremy
Spencer, and Danny Kirwan. One of the first
things Welch saw when he joined the group was
one of Jeremy's old suits hanging in the studio.*

BARE TREES
FLEETWOOD MAC

Produced: Fleetwood Mac.
(US) Reprise MS.2080. Released: March 1972.
(UK) Reprise K.44181. Released: August 1972.

Child Of Mine (Kirwan) Danny Kirwan vocal/**The Ghost** (Welch) Bob Welch vocal/**Homeward Bound** (McVie) Christine McVie vocal/**Sunny Side Of Heaven** (Kirwan) instrumental/**Bare Trees** (Kirwan) Danny Kirwan vocal/**Sentimental Lady** (Welch) Bob Welch vocal/**Danny's Chant** (Kirwan) Danny Kirwan vocal/**Spare Me A Little Of Your Love** (McVie) Christine McVie vocal/ **Dust** (Kirwan) Danny Kirwan vocal/**Thoughts On A Grey Day** (Mrs. Scarrot) narrative

Personnel:
Danny Kirwan (vocal, guitar), Bob Welch (vocal, guitar), Christine McVie (vocal, guitar), John McVie (bass), Mick Fleetwood (drums).

Talk about two steps forward, one step back!

Just when Fleetwood Mac had laid old ghosts to rest, and appeared to have overcome their identity crisis, Danny Kirwan started acting a little weird.

But then, what else can you expect from a Mac guitarman?

Kirwan's unexpected departure (October '72) was far less sensational than his former colleagues' exits. No God-bound moonlight flits or altruistic visions for Kirwan. "Danny," said Bob Welch later, "was just coming apart at the seams and couldn't function properly."

However, in official press statements circulated at the time, Kirwan's sacking was handled with kid-glove diplomacy. Rock's most clichéd copout, "differences of musical policy" was coughed up to save embarrassment.

Official word had it that Kirwan's music was getting further away from Mac's new direction and that he'd pulled out in order to pursue his own *destiny!*

Even the most superficial perusal of "Bare Trees" reveals no direction at all. Seemingly, all the work that had been poured into what was to be their '70s blueprint ("Future Games") came to nothing.

"Bare Trees" is a documentary of three erratic songwriters, each one working independently of the others. Worse still, there was no one at hand to tie together the loose knots.

At times, one gets the distinct impression that Danny, Bob and Christine were being tested to see who emerged as the strongest personality and who could be pushed to the fore. Paradoxically, all three singers appear reluctant to take on such responsibility. Or could it be that none of them possessed the necessary charisma?

Overall, "Bare Trees" is stilted and any high energy given off is feigned. Unlike the inspired "Future Games," this follow-up was in need of stringent arranging and editing.

Except for Welch's dewy-eyed "Sentimental Lady," the material is rather unexceptional, both Kirwan and McVie retreading well-worn ground. For the last time, the deposed guitarist reverts to his inevitable (though well-executed) guitar tremolo on "Sunny Side Of Heaven," reminiscent of Hank B. Marvin's "Wonderful Land." All that's missing is the maroon mohairs, fancy footwork and horn rims.

Christine McVie doesn't know whether to be soulful or introspective.

John and Mick press on regardless.

For all that, "Bare Trees" continued to further Fleetwood Mac's cause Stateside. Back

Danny Kirwan has quit Mac

DANNY KIRWAN has left Fleetwood Mac, and the group has been augmented by the introduction of two new members — they are Dave Walker (formerly with Savoy Brown) on vocals and Bob Weston (ex-Long John Baldry) on lead guitar. The new line-up have been in rehearsals for the past four weeks, and will make their debut in a European tour commencing in Scandinavia at the end of this month. They play Germany, Italy and Holland during the first 12 days of next month, and British dates are being set for the remainder of November. These will be followed in December by an American tour.

A spokesman for Mac told the NME: "Danny's music was getting further away from what Mac wanted to play. After spending a lot of time playing exhaustive tours of America, it was felt that new blood and fresh ideas were needed in the band. Danny was happy to leave, because he wanted to do a solo album for some time, and he is now working on this project".

Opposite page: *Like Peter Green and Jeremy Spencer before him, Danny Kirwan eventually left Fleetwood Mac.* Above: *There was considerable controversy over Kirwan's departure. The official word was that Kirwan had left of his own accord, but there were rumors he had been sacked.*

Snatched from "Bare Trees," Bob Welch's lilting "Sentimental Lady" is a low key smoocher ideal for that first furtive fumble. However, it was to take another five years for this song (re-recorded by the composer) to realize its full hit potential. (See page 113).

JEREMY SPENCER AND THE CHILDREN OF GOD
JEREMY SPENCER

Produced: Jeremy Spencer.
(US) Columbia KC.3I990. Released: November 8, 1972. (UK) CBS 69046. Released: September 21, 1973.

Can You Hear The Song (Spencer)/The World In Her Heart (Spencer)/Joan Of Arc (Spencer, Senek)/The Prophet (Spencer)/When I Looked To See The Sunshine (Spencer)/Let's Get On The Ball (Spencer)/Someone Told Me (Spencer, Senek)/Beauty For Ashes (Spencer, Senek)/War Horse (Spencer, Senek)/I Believe in Jesus (Spencer)

Personnel:
Jeremy Spencer (vocal, guitar, piano), Michael (vocal, guitar, harmonica), Phil Ham (guitar, flute, sitar), Moriah (vocal, tambourine), Boaz (vocal, bass, recorder), Ginnethon (drums, tablas, conga, tympani).

home, it was viewed as yet another nail in the coffin of Britain's Greatest Blues Band, where their sackclothed and ashed followers still mourned the original guitar triumvirate.

FLEETWOOD MAC

(A) Sentimental Lady (Welch) Bob Welch vocal/
(B) Sunny Side Of Heaven (Kirwan) instrumental

Produced: Fleetwood Mac.
(US) Reprise REP. 1093. Released: May 1972.
(UK) Not released.

Said Christine McVie of Bob Welch's addition to the music: "Bob has been instrumental in bringing us together as a group. He's like a breath of fresh air to us." Opposite page: After Danny Kirwan left, Bob Weston was added to the group as lead guitar. Left to right: Christine McVie, Mick Fleetwood, Bob Weston, Bob Welch, and (sitting) John McVie.

"It's awful," said Jeremy Spencer later, about this album of simpering God Rock. "It's horrible," he insisted. "For a start they mixed it on huge great speakers that had bags of treble. Finally, when the record was pressed, it had no presence at all. It was just like mud."

There's really nothing we can add!

PENGUIN
FLEETWOOD MAC

Produced: Fleetwood Mac and Martin Birch.
(US) Reprise MS:2138. Released: March 1973.
(UK) Reprise K.44235. Released: May 25,
1973.

Remember Me (McVie) Christine McVie vocal/
Bright Fire (Welch) Bob Welch vocal/**Dissatis-**
fied (McVie) Christine McVie vocal/**(I'm A) Road**
Runner (Holland, Dozier, Holland) Dave Walker
vocal/**The Derelict** (Walker) Dave Walker vocal/
Revelation (Welch) Bob Welch vocal/**Did You**
Ever Love Me (McVie, Welch) Christine McVie,
Bob Welch vocals/**Night Watch** (Welch) Bob
Welch vocal/**Caught In The Rain** (Weston)
instrumental

Personnel:
Bob Welch (vocal, guitar), **Bob Weston** (vocal,
guitar, slide guitar, harmonica), **Dave Walker**
(vocal, harmonica), **Christine McVie** (vocal,
keyboards), **John McVie** (bass), **Mick Fleetwood**
(drums, percussion).

Additional musicians:
Steve Nye (organ) "Night Watch," Ralph Rich-
ardson, Russel Valdez, Fred Totesaut (steel
drums) "Did You Ever Love Me".

Another day, another album, another lineup!

Singer Dave Walker and guitarist Bob
Weston had replaced the unfrocked Danny
Kirwan, but the Mac chemistry still wasn't
right.

Like Fleetwood Mac, the hirsute Walker had
earned his long service medals in various '60s
rock campaigns. Birmingham-based R & B
roughnecks the Redcaps gave Walker his first
break. Later, he replaced Jeff Lynne (of
Electric Light Orchestra fame) with the semi-
underground band the Idle Race before
taking over from Lonesome Dave (now with

Foghat) in the seemingly indestructible Savoy
Brown. Another Brit, Bob Weston entered
Mac's tradesmen's entrance direct from vet-
eran British R & B personality Long John
Baldry's band.

Such pedigree. Eat your heart out, Steely
Dan!

These two stalwarts were recruited for their
stolid down-to-earth qualities and because
they'd sunk a few beers backstage when
Baldry and Brown had toured with Mac.

Musicians have been hired for much less!

Walker's function was twofold—to give
Fleetwood Mac their badly needed onstage
focus and to swell their songbook. As "Penguin" makes only too clear, they'd chosen the
wrong man. Walker's contribution is confined
to just over seven minutes; a rework of Jr.
Walker's chestnut "(I'm A) Road Runner" and
one original, "The Derelict."

Mac 'Going Motown' just wasn't on. Equally
incongruous, Walker's own song sounds like
something rifled from Neil Young's trashcan.

Weston's "Caught In The Rain" was plain
anonymous, leaving Bob Welch and Christine
once again stuck in the hot seat.

Except for his coauthorship of "Did You Ever
Love Me," two of Welch's three compositions
were too stylized and compound his con-
fession that, "For the first couple of years I
was in the group, I really didn't know what I
was supposed to do." Only "Night Watch"
exudes genuine inspiration. Perhaps the un-
credited presence of one Peter Green may
have made Welch try harder. For once,
Welch's predilection for spacey studio effects
doesn't backfire on him. Block vocal harmonies are deftly overlayed with CSN & Y
tokin' textures.

Bob Weston lets loose on the guitar.

It took a woman to save the day. Christine McVie had finally found her niche. When it comes to writing melodies, Christine's imagination was somewhat limited to stock-in-trade devices but her material was often graced with a certain insidiousness. However, it's the way that she so effortlessly performs them that renders her songs quite irresistible. She knows how to exploit her talent to the fullest.

The chirpy opener "Remember Me," and the rumbustious "Dissatisfied" would have seemed perfectly in context on "Rumours" if given more cohesive arrangements. But "Penguin"'s gem (later culled as a single) is her collaboration with Bob Welch, "Did You Ever Love Me."

Though a transitional album, "Penguin" didn't impair Mac's American progress which continued, at a plodding pace.

N.B. Old John Barleycorn wasn't John McVie's only hobby. As an associated member of London's Zoological Society, he'd struck up a friendship with Regent's Park's penguin colony. "I didn't sit there and talk to them or anything like that, but I used to spend hours watching them." Love bloomed and John adopted a penguin as Fleetwood Mac's logo.

FLEETWOOD MAC

(A) Albatross (Green) instrumental/**(B) Need Your Love Tonight** (Spencer) Jeremy Spencer vocal

Produced: Mike Vernon.
(US) Not released. (UK) CBS 8306. Released: March 3, 1973.

And once again, the Ghost of Fleetwood Mac Past came to haunt the survivors, proving to be the proverbial albatross around the neck.

That may be, but the British public, with their short memory, immediately endorsed this re-release, sending "Albatross" to the giddy No. 2 slot on the charts.

To make matters worse, the "Penguin" lineup had overcome their paranoia about touring Britain, only to be inundated with requests for their "current" hit. Confusion was rife. "Top Of The Pops," running the original "Albatross" promo clip, got it wrong when the presenter announced to millions of viewers that Fleetwood Mac had broken up.

They say bad things come in threes and to further divert attention from Mac's '73 team, the rock press carried stories headlined: "PETER GREEN IS RECORDING AGAIN." According to these reports, circulated by Clifford Davis, Green had signed a six-album, three-year deal, the first album of which, scheduled for late summer release, was to be "Out Of Reach," a collection of material recorded in 1970. It never materialized. Neither did the remaining five.

FLEETWOOD MAC

(A) Remember Me (McVie) Christine McVie vocal/**(B) Dissatisfied** (McVie) Christine McVie vocal

Produced: Fleetwood Mac and Martin Birch.
(US) Reprise REP.1159. Released: May 16, 1973. (UK) Not released.

Mac's music was right for American consumption, but they still had strong misgivings about Britain, where Glitter Rock was at its zenith and bands like Roxy Music ruled.

Their fears weren't without foundation.

Dave Walker during a 1973 concert.

Mick Fleetwood pauses for a break during a recording session.

once again found singles form.

For all its tropical atmosphere (Bacardi & Coke steel drummers doing their Caribbean Cruise sales pitch), the song's well-metered melody glides in a way that is reminiscent of those classic Smokey Robinson velvet-gloved soul ballads.

Obviously, two heads were better than one. Why Fleetwood Mac didn't further exploit this partnership is beyond comprehension. The group were forced to wait what seemed like an eternity before producing another single of this calibre.

FLEETWOOD MAC

(A) Black Magic Woman (Green) Peter Green vocal/**(B) Stop Messin' 'Round** (Green, Adams) Peter Green vocal

Produced: Mike Vernon.
(US) Not released. (UK) CBS 1722. Released: August 17, 1973.

If CBS thought they were going to enjoy a string of hits with Mac oldies they were in for a rude awakening. "Fleetwood Mac doing a Santana number, eh?"

FLEETWOOD MAC

(A) Did You Ever Love Me (McVie, Welch) Christine McVie, Bob Welch vocals/**(B) Revelation** (Welch)

Produced: Fleetwood Mac and Martin Birch.
(US) Reprise REP.1172. Released: August 29, 1973. (UK) Not released.

Stateside, Bob Welch's "Revelation" was chosen as the flip in preference to Dave Walker's "The Derelict."

FLEETWOOD MAC

(A) Did You Ever Love Me (McVie, Welch) Christine McVie, Bob Welch vocals/**(B) The Derelict** (Walker) Dave Walker vocal

Produced: Fleetwood Mac and Martin Birch.
(US) Not released. (UK) Reprise K.14280. Released June 22, 1973.

A one-off Christine McVie-Bob Welch collaboration (first heard on the "Penguin" album), the buoyant "Did You Ever Love Me" gave the distinct impression that Fleetwood Mac had

John and Christine McVie were soon to learn that marriage and music didn't mix.

Stevie Nicks and Lindsey Buckingham were a musical and romantic team for quite some time. They released their first album together in 1973.

BUCKINGHAM NICKS
LINDSEY BUCKINGHAM/STEVIE NICKS

Produced: Keith Olsen.
Executive Producer: Richard Dashut.
(US) Polydor D.5058. Released: September 5, 1973. (UK) Polydor 2391093. Released: February 1977.

Crying In The Night (Nicks)/**Stephanie** (Buckingham)/**Without A Leg To Stand On** (Buckingham)/**Crystal** (Nicks)/**Long Distance Winner** (Nicks)/**Don't Let Me Down Again** (Buckingham)/**Django** (Lewis)/**Races Are Run** (Nicks)/**Lola (My Love)** (Buckingham)/**Frozen Love** (Nicks, Buckingham)

This album marks the inauspicious debut of two romantically linked and ambitious young American singer-songwriters, no better or worse than countless others looking for a break.

If anything, other than the provocative sleeve, stood out from this mildly derivative milk-tooth collection, it's the unusual nasal timbre of the *prettier* half of this self-consciously liberated boy-girl duo, Stevie Nicks.

But it was to take two years for anyone to notice this asset, save for an incongruous cult following Buckingham & Nicks had picked up in the South—where rock audiences were usually more partial to booze-drenched thuggery than anything as restrained as this.

Buckingham & Nicks were big, but big, in Birmingham, Alabama.

Each came straight from the heart of the American Dream. Buckingham was born and raised comfortably in Atherton near Palo Alto, 30 miles south of San Francisco. His family were sports nuts. A brother won an Olympic Silver Medal in 1968 for aquasport.

Lindsey also had webbed feet; he was a keen water polo player. When his fingers weren't wrinkled he slaved away at the guitar, an instrument he began playing at an early age.

Buckingham's elder brother's extensive record collection acted as a vast source of inspiration and reference for the fledgling musician. "It was like having the story of rock 'n' roll unfurled in front of me," he said. "My brother used to come home with all these classic rock singles...Elvis, Buddy Holly, The Everly Brothers, Chuck Berry and Eddie Cochran."

Having absorbed '50s rock, he developed a liking for folk and bluegrass, working out picking styles on acoustic guitar. But Buckingham's musical aspirations were strictly amateur. "Even all through high school, I would go watch bands, and even though I probably played guitar better than people who were up there, I was just doing it for fun," he remembered.

Even so, Buckingham's electric guitar technique wasn't that far advanced, for when, in 1967, he joined his first professional band, Fritz, he was transferred to bass, since he found it extremely difficult to master the then fashionable heavy rock style.

From the outset Stevie (Stephanie) Nicks has never been one to compromise, ingenue though she might appear.

"The star in my family sky," Stevie, the only daughter of a high-powered businessman, was born in Phoenix, Arizona. The Nickses moved around a lot during their beloved daughter's childhood, living in Los Angeles, New Mexico, Texas and Utah, as the head of the family made it to the top; at one time

Stevie's father was simultaneously first-and second-in-command of Armour Meats and Greyhound respectively.

Her grandfather, Aaron Jeff Nicks, hadn't done so well.

A luckless country & western singer who knew his way around too many a hangover, he died a bitter and unfulfilled performer.

Stevie learned to sing at his knee.

In her teens, she learned even more from Phil Spector's "Little Symphonies For The Kiddies" and such sublime song-orientated bands as the Byrds and Buffalo Springfield, and, at 16, began writing her own material.

She studied speech communication at San Jose State University, but quit before graduating, much against her parents' wishes, to sing with Fritz, where she encountered Buckingham for the first time.

Completing the lineup were Xavier Pacheco (organ, vocals), Brian Kane (guitar) and Bob Geary (drums). Stevie had been invited to join by Kane whom she'd met at a Young Life meeting in high school. The meeting resulted in the two performing an impromptu version of "California Dreamin'."

Fritz, in Stevie's own words, were, "a riff-oriented quasi-acid rock band" that played around the Bay Area clubs. They only made it onto the major bills when they opened for the likes of Santana, Hendrix and, more relevantly, Janis Joplin.

Seeing Joplin at her peak was an experience of satori-style proportions for the impressionable 18-year-old Nicks, then playing her third professional gig.

"You couldn't have pried me away with a million-dollar check," remembered Nicks, who that night in her nylons, miniskirt and T-strap shoes cut a radical contrast to Joplin's outrageous sexual histrionics.

"I was absolutely glued to her. It was there that I learned a lot of what to do onstage. It wasn't that I wanted to look like Joplin, because I didn't. But I said, 'If ever I am a performer of any value, I want to be able to create the same kind of feeling that's going on between her and her audience.'"

To keep things strictly on a businesslike basis, Fritz enforced a "Hands Off Stevie Nicks" policy. Not that anyone wanted to know anyway; her ambitious nature unsettled her male colleagues. As Stevie said herself, "Being the female singer out front, the focal point, I got a lot of attention, even if I didn't deserve it. The band wasn't amused by this."

Though for this reason the boys in the band never took Stevie all that seriously, it was her natural foxiness which drew in the promoters. Around San Francisco, Fritz were invariably referred to as "The band with the brownish-blondish haired girl."

Nicks Appeal still wasn't enough to hoist Fritz from the local lower echelons, or, come to that, land them a record deal. Though Fritz boasted an original repertoire, it excluded anything penned by either Buckingham or Nicks. It wasn't until Fritz disbanded in 1971, that Buckingham and Nicks were given the opportunity to explore their embryonic song-writing talents.

Now that interband pressures no longer existed, Lindsey didn't waste any time in establishing a more personal relationship with the Phoenix Belle. Just as the two of them were about to move south to Los Angeles, where they reckoned to stand a better chance of achieving their ambitions, Buckingham was

Stevie claims that she "learned a lot of what to do on stage" from the legendary Janis Joplin.

When Lindsey Buckingham came down with mononucleosis, he and Stevie had to postpone their musical careers for almost a year. But the illness did enable Lindsey to spend more time perfecting his technique on the electric guitar.

struck down with mononucleosis (glandular fever), and the duo had to postpone their plans for almost a year.

The illness did, however, enable Lindsey to develop his technique on electric guitar and the two to work out some preliminary demos. On arrival in L.A. they secured a record deal through a friend, Keith Olsen, with a local custom label Anthem. The idea was to fly the duo to London to record at Trident Studios.

This was aborted when Anthem's owners fell out after a fight. The label went out of business permanently while Buckingham & Nicks were to be grounded, temporarily.

Fortunately, one of Anthem's owners, Lee LaSaffe, got a job with Polydor Records' New York office and was responsible for this album being made.

Old Pals can only get you so far, for Polydor failed to pick up the option on a second album and Buckingham & Nicks were once again label-less.

To pay the rent, Buckingham hustled ads over the phone for a nonexistent business products directory, or turned to session work. He toured with Don Everly's backup band, singing Phil's vocal parts for the Greatest Hits medley. Meanwhile, Stevie waited tables for $1.50 an hour in Clementine's, a then-fashionable '20s-style singles rendezvous in Hollywood.

Buckingham & Nicks hadn't ditched their recording aspirations, but nobody was killed in the stampede to cut a second album.

20th Century Records' Russ Regan liked what he heard but he didn't act on it. Poker-faced Ode Records' boss Lou Adler palmed them off with the obligatory "don't-call-us-we'll-call-you" routine before the first song was halfway through. The final insult came when one "starmaker" suggested they xerox the Top 40 and hit the steak-and-lobster circuit.

The latter might have provided some solace, since the destitute duo, particularly Stevie, was becoming not a little emaciated. When she visited home, the anxious Nickses saw in their ebullient daughter an unnerving shadow of her late grandfather.

The two American singers had a large fan following, especially in the South.

Stevie was taught how to sing by her grandfather, a luckless country and western singer. However, in the early stages of her career, Stevie was valued more for her looks than her voice.

MYSTERY TO ME
FLEETWOOD MAC

Produced: Fleetwood Mac and Martin Birch. (US) Reprise MS.2158. Released: October 15, 1973. (UK) Reprise K.44248. Released: January 11,1974.

Emerald Eyes (Welch) Bob Welch vocal/**Believe Me** (McVie) Christine McVie vocal/**Just Crazy Love** (McVie) Christine McVie vocal/**Hypnotized** (Welch) Bob Welch vocal/**Forever** (Weston, McVie, Welch)/**Keep On Going** (Welch) Christine McVie vocal/**In The City** (Welch) Bob Welch vocal/**Miles Away** (Welch) Bob Welch vocal/**Somebody** (Welch) Bob Welch vocal/**The Way I Feel** (McVie) Christine McVie vocal/**For Your Love** (Gouldman) Bob Welch vocal/**Why** (McVie) Christine McVie vocal

Personnel:
Bob Welch (vocal, guitar), **Bob Weston** (lead & slide guitar), **Christine McVie** (vocal, keyboards), **John McVie** (bass), **Mick Fleetwood** (drums).

During the recording of "Mystery To Me," Fleetwood Mac faced up to the fact that Dave Walker just had to go. After cutting two tracks (according to Walker, "the best thing I've ever done") the singer from whom they'd expected too much was dumped.

His employers' decision wasn't unexpected. Walker was aware of the others' growing resentment over his inability to either hack it in the spotlight or contribute to their repertoire. The result was that both McVie and Welch not only had to write for themselves, but also for a passenger. And Walker's highly restricted guts 'n' glory, blues and boogie style wasn't the direction they had in mind.

Things reached the point of no return when, in Walker's hands, Welch's "Hypnotized"

turned out as a dated blues. "We sounded like Savoy Brown," Welch recollected none too fondly.

A fresh start was made—sans Walker.

At this rickety stage in their traumatic career, the process of making an album was, for Fleetwood Mac, akin to paying penance. Like so many other bands seemingly past their peak and fighting for survival, the Mac were contracted to produce records whether or not they had anything remotely worth saying in public.

"Mystery To Me" is all style and practically no content. Whatever personality they once had was no longer evident.

N.B. Two weeks before the album's release, one song, "Good Things" was dropped. "For Your Love" was substituted, but as 50,000 sleeves were already printed, "Good Things" is still listed on a considerable proportion of copies of this LP.

In November '77, David Walker was announced as Ozzy Osbourne's replacement in Black Sabbath. Two months later, Walker had been ousted—Osbourne had rejoined.

BUCKINGHAM NICKS

(A) Don't Let Me Down Again (Buckingham)/**(B) Races Are Run** (Nicks)

Produced: Keith Olsen.
Executive Producer: Richard Dashut.
(US) Polydor PD.14209. Released: November 2, 1973. (UK) Not released.

The first of several Buckingham & Nicks tracks to be peeled from the album. The LP in fact only comprised nine tracks proper, a tenth being a truncated acoustic guitar interpretation of The Modern Jazz Quartet's immortal "Django."

"Don't Let Me Down Again" is characteristic of Buckingham's fixation with the kind of guitar gymnastics and rock styles perpetrated at the beginning of the '70s by blue-eyed soulsters Delaney & Bonnie and Friends (of which Eric Clapton was the most prominent).

Really, it's a case of unfulfilled potential. Buckingham's ideas and performance are by no means slipshod. Just that the lack of any presence in the production and the overt absence of any dynamics in the rhythm section prevent it from being the flame-out rocker it was obviously envisioned to be.

Given the Fleetwood Mac facelift, particularly Fleetwood's incendiary drums, the song would have easily charted. Buckingham's only consolation was that it was covered no less than four times. "Races Are Run" is redolent of a love theme from a low-budget Hollywood "youth market" movie.

"Don't Let Me Down Again" is frequently used as one of Fleetwood Mac's encores.

FLEETWOOD MAC

(A) For Your Love (Gouldman) Bob Welch vocal/**(B) Hypnotized** (Welch) Bob Welch vocal

Produced: Fleetwood Mac.
(US) Reprise REP.1188. Released: December 12, 1973. (UK) Reprise K.14315. Released: March 8, 1974.

Doubtful of the chart potential of any of the tracks on "Mystery To Me," Mac bowed to Bob Weston's suggestion to re-record The Yardbirds' 1965 hit, "For Your Love."

The B-side, "Hypnotized," is still Bob

Welch's best-known Mac track. It's persistently featured on late Saturday night FM-radio shows. Along with "Did You Ever Love Me," the most broadcast of all post-Green/pre-B&N Fleetwood Mac cuts.

BUCKINGHAM NICKS

(A) Crying In The Night (Nicks)/**(B) Without A Leg to Stand On** (Buckingham)

Produced: Keith Olsen.
Executive Producer: Richard Dashut.
(US) Polydor PD.14229. Released: February 14, 1974. (UK) Not released.

Influences abound on this St. Valentine's Day release, as both Buckingham & Nicks demonstrate their singer-songwriter roots. Stevie's song, a mid-tempo acoustic strumalong, owes more than a nod to Joni Mitchell's "Blue." The chord progression is a major variation of the minor rundowns she used in "California" and "A Case Of You."

Buckingham's influence is not so close to home—"Without A Leg To Stand On" would have sounded entirely in context on Cat Stevens' "Teaser And The Firecat" album.

BUCKINGHAM NICKS

(A) Don't Let Me Down Again (Buckingham)/**(B) Crystal** (Nicks)

Produced: Keith Olsen.
Executive Producer: Richard Dashut.
(US) Not released. (UK) Polydor 2066077. Released: April 1974.

Though "Don't Let Me Down Again" was first released in America November 2, 1973 (see

During his stay with Fleetwood Mac, Bob Welch contributed twenty original songs and collaborated on another three.

page 82), this was Buckingham & Nicks' first UK release. The familiar A-side was coupled with the ethereal "Crystal," a song owing much to David Crosby.

Later, there were two perfunctory re-issues: (UK) July 23, 1976. (US) Polydor PD.14428. September 21, 1977.

HEROES ARE HARD TO FIND
FLEETWOOD MAC

Produced: Fleetwood Mac and Bob Hughes. (US) Reprise MS.2196. Released: September 10, 1974. (UK) Reprise K.54026. Released: September 13, 1974.

Heroes Are Hard To Find (McVie) Christine McVie vocal/**Coming Home** (Welch) Bob Welch vocal/**Angel** (Welch) Bob Welch vocal/**Bermuda Triangle** (Welch) Bob Welch vocal/**Come A Little Bit Closer** (McVie) Christine McVie vocal/**She's Changing Me** (Welch) Bob Welch vocal/**Bad Loser** (McVie) Christine McVie vocal/**Silver Heels** (Welch) Bob Welch vocal/**Prove Your Love** (McVie) Christine McVie vocal/**Born Enchanter** (Welch) Bob Welch vocal/**Safe Harbor** (Welch) instrumental

Personnel:
Bob Welch (vocal, guitar, vibraphone), Christine McVie (vocal, keyboards), John McVie (bass), Mick Fleetwood (drums, percussion).

Additional musicians:
Pete Kleinow (pedal steel guitar) "Come A Little Bit Closer" Nick De Caro (string and horn arrangements).

The sequence of events surrounding the making of this, Bob Welch's last album with Fleetwood Mac, looked for a time so serious that it could well have been the *group's* last album!

Dirty work was afoot.

Mick Fleetwood, his wife Jenny (sister of ex-Beatle bride Patti Boyd), and Mac's almost invisible second guitarist Bob Weston were involved in an eternal triangle. Such was the animosity between Fleetwood and Weston that it threatened to rip the group asunder. By October 1973, it had become impossible for the two musicians to work together on the same stage.

It was backstage in Lincoln, Nebraska, when Fleetwood admitted that he couldn't take the emotional strain any longer. The group's usually unflappable drummer requested the remainder of the tour be cancelled. So it was, and a three month cooling-off period was mutually agreed upon.

During the layoff, the by now Weston-less Fleetwood Mac were beset with more problems. Talk about pouring salt on wounds.

It was Christmas '73, when Welch was astounded to hear from American promoters calling to say how pleased they were the band was back in action. It only took a few more calls to learn that in Mac's absence, manager Clifford Davis had claimed control of the name *Fleetwood Mac* and was intending to put a band *called* Fleetwood Mac out on the road.

Davis felt that he was originally responsible for launching the band and molding its career. In this light, he felt entitled to shape the personnel of *any* group called Fleetwood Mac.

Fleetwood, Welch, and the McVies didn't accept Davis' point of view—or his letters offering each a place in the new lineup. So when Davis shoved Elmer Gantry, Rick Kirby, Paul Martinez, David Wilkinson and Craig Collinge onto the US tour circuit carrying

Opposite page: *Rock history was made when Cliff Davis launched a bogus boogie band with Fleetwood Mac's name. The release ot "Heroes" was stalled by Davis's legal machinations. Above: Bob Weston left in 1973 because of personal problems within the group. Weston's interest in Mick Fleetwood's wife made it impossible for the two musicians to be on stage together.*

Mac back – after year of wrangles

FLEETWOOD MAC have been granted an injunction in the Chancery Division of the High Court, preventing anyone other than the members of the original group — Mick Fleetwood, John McVie, Bob Welch and Christine McVie — from operating under the name of Fleetwood Mac. The order was made against the band's former manager Clifford Davis and the three musicians who have veen working under his aegis as Fleetwood Mac in the States — Elmer Gantry, Paul Martinez and Rick Kirby.

The original Mac have not worked in public since last October, during which time they have been awaiting the outcome of legal wrangles over the existence of two Fleetwood Mac groups. As reported by NME in February, Davis formed the new band on the grounds — he claimed — that he had been responsible for launching the outfit in the first place, and was therefore entitled to shape the personnel of any group named fleetwood Mac.

Now Mick Fleetwood and his three colleagues have the field to themselves. They are at present in Angeles, where they have ... new album for ... rs, and are at ng for a lengthy ... which is due to ... r 1 "to help repair ... one by the other

... pokesman for Mac ... k: "There has been ... w to prevent the ori- ... from working for the ... but they felt it advis- ... ain in the background ... ther 'bogus' group was ... while tne ... touring and while legal action was pending. Now the restraining order has been granted, and this will last until the action comes to trial — which may not be for a year or two, although I feel the final outcome will be the same. The original Mac also intend to sue Clifford Davis for damages."

Mac all clear

FLEETWOOD MAC's new album "Heroes Are Hard To Find" will, after all, be going on sale within the next two weeks. This is the result of Warner Brothers winning their appeal against the injunction, secured by Mac's former manager Clifford Davis, which had restrained them from selling the album.

Fleetwood Mac's battle standard, the *real* Fleetwood Mac stood up and filed suit.

As is uaually the case in such disputes, stories greatly contradict. Rick Kirby has it that Mick Fleetwood had sometime during the three month layoff instructed Davis to reform the band which he would lead. Two weeks before the first American dates Fleetwood opted out. Welch vehemently denies this version.

Litigation was protracted and extremely costly. If the band were something less than solvent prior to the dispute, nine months of five-day-a-week visits to their legal eagles (Davenport & Lyons) left them almost bankrupt. Their counsel advised them to stay off the road so no gig money was coming in. To add to the nightmare, at one point they felt the case was going against them.

Concurrent with the legal hassles the band finally moved from England to live in Los Angeles. Fleetwood had wanted to base the band on the West Coast a year before. It was an expensive piece of business commuting across the Atlantic to work. On settling in California, Fleetwood Mac renegotiated their Warner-Reprise recording contract and set about clearing their name, soiled by the bogus band's critically savaged concert performances.

There was no shortage of managers wishing to represent the band, even if some were audacious enough to suggest a change of name. Once bitten, twice shy, Mick Fleetwood, with the assistance of John McVie and Bob Welch, decided to keep the job in the family. Despite the misgivings of Warner-Reprise, Mick Fleetwood personally took over the management of Fleetwood Mac.

Davis, a man not to give up easily, delayed the release of "Heroes Are Hard To Find" with a court injunction, subsequently overruled by Mac's appeal. Whether the result of their courtroom dramas, or just that the band had exhausted a not particularly bountiful seam, this album is, at the time they needed it most, their most uninspired effort to date.

Fleetwood Mac weren't aware of the record's shortcomings. Quite the contrary. Optimistic of their immediate future, they once more headed on down the Great American Highway—though this time anticipating that the new album would be a sure-fire smash comeback.

It was not to be.

Welch, who'd hung in there longer than any other guitarist, couldn't take it any more. The fact that he was experiencing marital upheavals only worsened things. Though Welch contributed seven songs, he was now running dry. "I didn't have another song in me left to write and now I was going downhill very, very fast," he said.

And sadly it shows. Welch's material meanders between quasi-jazzy psychedelics and untethered guitar atmospherics which vainly attempt to recapture former glories. "Safe Harbor," for instance, is nothing but a pale shadow of "Albatross." Once again Christine McVie is their trump card. But even when she assumes the spotlight, it's still a fight to infuse any degree of vitality.

The overall impression is that "Heroes" sounds like it was made as an afterthought, a contractual obligation. "Heroes Are Hard To Find." So are ideas.

At Christmas Bob Welch quit.

FLEETWOOD MAC

(A) **Heroes Are Hard To Find** (McVie) Christine McVie vocal/(B) **Born Enchanter** (Welch) Bob Welch vocal

Produced: Fleetwood Mac and Bob Hughes. (US) Reprise REP.1317. Released: November 20, 1974. (UK) Reprise K.14388. Released: February 1975.

So too, it seems, were hit singles!

FLEETWOOD MAC
FLEETWOOD MAC

Produced: Fleetwood Mac and Keith Olsen. (US) Reprise MS.2225. Released: July 11, 1975. (UK) Reprise K.54043. Released: August 1975.

Monday Morning (Buckingham) Lindsey Buckingham vocal/**Warm Ways** (McVie) Christine McVie vocal/**Blue Letter** (Curtis) Lindsey Buckingham vocal/**Rhiannon** (Nicks) Stevie Nicks vocal/**Over My Head** (McVie) Christine McVie vocal/**Crystal** (Nicks) Lindsey Buckingham, Stevie Nicks vocals/**Say You Love Me** (McVie) Christine McVie vocal/**Landslide** (Nicks) Stevie Nicks vocal/**World Turning** (McVie, Buckingham) Lindsey Buckingham vocal/**Sugar Daddy** (McVie) Christine McVie vocal/**I'm So Afraid** (Buckingham) Lindsey Buckingham vocal

Personnel:
Stevie Nicks (vocal), Lindsey Buckingham (vocal, guitar), Christine McVie (vocal, keyboards), John McVie (bass), Mick Fleetwood (drums).
Additional musicians:
Waddy (rhythm guitar), "Sugar Daddy."

Let's not get *too* mystical about this, but facts are facts. With the casual introduction of Lindsey Buckingham and Stevie Nicks, Fleet-wood Mac had returned to a lineup that once again boasted a front line of three autonomous singer-composers.

Not since the halcyon hit-making era of Green, Spencer and Kirwan, had Fleetwood Mac been able to tap such resources. The band had not only gone full circle, so to speak, but the chemistry was once again of galvanic proportions.

Can you believe this? Buckingham and Nicks didn't even need to physically audition for the eleventh installment in Fleetwood Mac's lurid saga. It was almost like a scene out of an old MGM musical—two bright-eyed young things stumble into a theatre and without a rehearsal save the show on opening night.

Moreover, it wasn't as if the desperate duo were clutching for the nearest lifeline. "Stevie and I," said the juvenile lead, "really weren't ecstatic about Mick's offer to join Fleetwood Mac, because we really believed in what we were doing with our second album."

For their part, Mick Fleetwood and John McVie had long ago learned to expect the worst. If "The White Album," as the band subsequently referred to it, had proved to be yet another mediocre seller, and the kids hadn't worked out, they'd have stoically sought replacements and ploughed on regardless. British reserve and all that, what!

For a change, Mick Fleetwood wasn't looking for replacements when he inadvertently ran across Buckingham and Nicks. He was cruisin' L.A. looking for a suitable studio in which to record the next Mac album. Arriving at Sound City in Van Nuys, studio engineer Keith Olsen played Fleetwood a tape of Buckingham and Nicks' "Frozen Love"

Mac: Welch goes, second girl joins

FLEETWOOD MAC have lost guitarist Bob Welch, who has left the band to concentrate on production work. And he has been replaced in the line-up by two new members — Stevie Nicks (who, despite the name, is in fact a girl) and guitarist Lindsey ... sey ... chan... have...

tine McVie and newcomer Stevie.
It is not yet clear how Mac will be affected by this new policy, although it would seem to point to a change in their musical approach. The band are now based permanently in Los Angeles, where they are currently engaged in cutting a new album — which ...duced by their former

Mac gigging soon

FLEETWOOD MAC are planning a full British and European tour in the early summer. They undertake a month-long U.S. itinerary from May 15, and intend to start working on this side of the Atlantic as soon as they have completed their American commitments. As reported by NME eight weeks ago, Mac have undergone a personnel change with the departure of lead guitarist Bob Welch. He has been replaced in the line-up by guitarist Lindsey Buckingham and girl vocalist ... Hicks, which means that — with Christine M... ... two girl singers. Says Mick... ... almost ...

Opposite page: *The real Mac won the legal fight!* Above: *Mac added Stevie Nicks and Lindsey Buckingham to the group in 1975.*

John McVie, Lindsey Buckingham, Christine McVie, Stevie Nicks, and Mick Fleetwood. Mick hired Stevie and Lindsey without an audition.

to simply demonstrate the studio's recording facilities.

Next door, the duo themselves were routining demos for what was intended as their second album. Hearing their own work blasting over the playback speakers in the adjacent studio, a curious Lindsey Buckingham went out to investigate. He discovered the campanile drummer vigorously flexing his feet muscles. An introduction was effected.

Time passed. Material for the upcoming Fleetwood Mac album, their eleventh, was being written, when suddenly Bob Welch, dearly beloved by his long-standing comrades, quit. Panic stations....

Now where the hell did Mick Fleetwood put those tousle-haired kids' phone number?

It was New Year's Eve, when Keith Olsen informed Lindsey and Stevie that Fleetwood was hiring and they were his first choice.

The songbirds accepted, but first they had one outstanding commitment—their biggest headlining gig as a duo before a rapturous sellout crowd of 7,000 in Birmingham, Alabama. That over, some quick rehearsals, followed by ten days in Sound City Studios, and "The White Album" was in the can.

Such brevity in recording what is, on any level, a highly polished LP, is because most of the material had been written prior to this new alliance: "Crystal" first appeared on the solitary Buckingham & Nicks album, while "Monday Morning," "Landslide" and "Rhiannon" had already been demoed for the two's curtailed follow-up. Seemingly, only Buckingham-McVie's "World Turning" stems from the actual sessions.

The LP was called "Fleetwood Mac," and not some less overt catchphrase, so as to re-

emphasize the group's continuity, despite the sudden personnel upheaval.

In time-honored fashion, the thoroughly revitalized Fleetwood Mac went out on the road for a solid six months to make or break this album. It wasn't until a single, Christine McVie's luxuriant "Over My Head," had given them their first major American hit, that the album started selling faster than it could be re-pressed.

Visually and aurally, Fleetwood Mac had suddenly become exceedingly attractive to AM radio-orientated audiences. The grafting of Buckingham and Nicks into the band immediately stimulated the battle-weary rhythm section and paradoxically, at long last, gave Christine McVie the opportunity to fully

Soon after Stevie and Lindsey joined Mac, the group hit the top of the pop charts with the release of "Fleetwood Mac."

Introverted Christine McVie enjoys sharing the limelight with the flashier Stevie Nicks.

realize her potential, even if she wasn't aware of it herself.

Regarding herself as the counterpoint to Nicks' coquettish feline flash, Christine admitted self-consciously, "It's great because Stevie is a show-woman and she loves it. I'm the keyboard player which keeps me out of the limelight. I enjoy it because I'm not an extrovert."

Not only did Christine begin to strike up a rapport chatting to audiences between numbers; it was her songs that gave this new band its initial chart impetus.

Three of the four singles extracted from "The White Album" were McVie originals, sung with more conviction than she'd been able to muster before. "The White Album," however, shouldn't be misconstrued as a one-woman showcase. Not since their chart-busting singles days had Mac displayed such a cohesive identity on record and onstage.

Stevie Nicks wasn't kidding when she said of the first time all five met (at Mick Fleetwood's Laurel Canyon home), "Did you ever meet someone where you sit down and talk to them and immediately feel like you've known them for a long time?"

"The White Album" exhibits genuine group empathy. The band no longer appear to treat each other's songs purely as solo vehicles—the singer upfront, the remainder working unobtrusively in the shadows.

It's the pop-rock sensibility of this album which distinguishes it from its predecessors; Fleetwood Mac had never sounded like this before. Arrangements are meticulously crafted, hooklines proliferate, vocal harmonies—previously absent—abound, and enthusiasm is at an all-time premium.

In much the same way as the first Crosby, Stills & Nash album introduced a refreshing vocal harmony sound—one differing from surrogate Beatle structures, "The White Album" offers an alternative to all those West Coast cowboy fixated rock bands of which the Eagles are the apothesis. The two contrasting voices of McVie and Nicks, together with Buckingham's dry tenor, create instantly recognizable vocal textures.

As for the material, it's a combination of the more traditional aspects of British High Pop, ever so subtly deployed Beatleisms, and the best aspects of California gloss; the whole is greater than the sum of the parts. This is consistently driven by one of the most reliable rhythm sections since Wyman and Watts.

"The White Album" is immediately accessible and like mid-period Beatle albums, and more recently, Elton John's "Goodbye Yellow Brick Road," appeals to the widest possible crossover audience. It's no use having the ingredients on record unless you can project them in person. Fleetwood Mac, now with added sex appeal, were once more a dynamic onstage combo, each band member defining a clear-cut personal identity.

The American contingent, Buckingham & Nicks, resplendent in their finery, were the perfect foil for the less flamboyant Britishers. Like The Stones' Bill Wyman, John McVie barely moves a muscle onstage, let alone smiles, preferring to hang back near Fleetwood's quietly dazzling drums. Christine too rarely ventures beyond her modest bank of keyboards.

Buckingham & Nicks are easy for their American audiences to identify with. Each looks well-laundered and successful, and yet not too distant from those who've paid to see them, like the Stevie Nicks lookalikes with their shag haircuts and slightly upmarket, hippyish threads.

Fleetwood Mac were no longer anonymous.

"The White Album" pursued an eccentric path to success. It reached as high as number nine and dropped to 40 before it regained its upward curve.

FLEETWOOD MAC

(A) *Man Of The World (Green) Peter Green vocal

DANNY KIRWAN

(B) **Second Chapter (Kirwan) Danny Kirwan vocal

Produced: *Fleetwood Mac **Martin Rushent. (US) Not released. (UK) DJM DJS.10620. Released: October 24, 1975.

The third appearance of this Mac classic on a different label and with a different B-side. Seemingly, its commerciality had long since been exhausted!

FLEETWOOD MAC

(A) Warm Ways (McVie) Christine McVie vocal/ (B) Blue Letter (Curtis) Lindsey Buckingham vocal

Produced: Fleetwood Mac and Keith Olsen. (US) Not released. (UK) Reprise K.14403. Released: October 24, 1975.

Could be that Christine caught one too many reruns of Elvis' "Blue Hawaii" on the late late show, because "Warm Ways," the first single plucked from "The White Album," positively drips Polynesian tranquility.

One can almost picture the songstress, sitting demurely at the keyboards, lei around her neck, a pineapple punch within easy reach, crooning this gentle lullabye against a spectacular Pacific sunset.

Despite its gossamer grace, it was an odd choice for a single, considering the number of "obvious" hit singles "The White Album" harbored.

Very much in The Eagles "Take It Easy" mold, "Blue Letter" heads on down the highway at a fair clip with Buckingham hogging the microphone and unraveling ribbons of lengthy fuzz-jangle guitar.

FLEETWOOD MAC

(A) Over My Head (McVie) Christine McVie vocal/(B) I'm So Afraid (Buckingham) Lindsey Buckingham vocal

Produced: Fleetwood Mac and Keith Olsen. (US) Reprise RPS.1339. Released: September 24, 1975. (UK) Reprise K.14413. Released: February 13, 1976.

The infectious rhythm guitar pattern upon which the Doobie Brothers built their career, with hits like "Long Train Runnin'" and "Listen To The Music," is here given yet another airing.

This time around, however, the familiar lick is characteristically, for a Christine McVie song, understated. Along with "Say You Love Me" (later to do even better chartwise), Christine composed "Over My Head" on a portable Hohner piano in the bedroom of a small three-room Malibu apartment the McVies moved into when they set up home in L.A.

Says Christine of Stevie's on-stage personality: "She's a show woman and she loves it."

Danny Kirwan resurrected some ex-Chicken Shack members for his solo debut.

Adverse criticism in the American press had added to Stevie Nicks' (who sings harmony on this single) self-doubt. Prior to the runaway success of "Over My Head," she was on the verge of leaving the band.

As for the B-side...had Lindsey Buckingham been digging out all those old Mac hits like "Green Manalishi," or maybe listening to Redbone? Anyway, though he got the backing track right, he picked the wrong key to sing "I'm So Afraid" in.

DANNY KIRWAN

(A) Ram Jam City (Kirwan)/**(B) Hot Summer's Day** (Kirwan)

Produced: Martin Rushent.
(US) DJM DJUS.1004. Released: November 11, 1975. (UK) DJM DJS.396. Released: July 25, 1975.

Kirwan's first solo single. A folksy opus replete with mandolin and fiddle, it perhaps explains one of the reasons why Kirwan was asked to leave Mac. A hit it wasn't.

A week after its British release, "Ram Jam City" re-appeared with a new B-side, "Angel's Delight," and new catalogue number—DJM DJS.10709.

SECOND CHAPTER
DANNY KIRWAN

Produced: Martin Rushent.
(US) DJM DJL.PA-I. Released: November 18, 1975. (UK) DJM DJF.20454. Released: September 12, 1975.

Ram Jam City (Kirwan)/**Odds And Ends** (Kirwan)/**Hot Summer's Day** (Kirwan)/**Mary Jane** (Kirwan)/**Skip A Dee Doo** (Kirwan)/**Love Can Al-**

ways Bring You Happiness (Kirwan)/**Second Chapter** (Kirwan)/**Lovely Days** (Kirwan)/**Falling In Love With You** (Kirwan)/**Silver Stream** (Kirwan)/**Best Girl In The World** (Kirwan)/**Cascades** (Kirwan)

Personnel:
Danny Kirwan (vocal, guitars), **Paul Raymond** (piano), **Andy Silvester** (bass), **Geoff Britton** (drums), **Jim Russell** (drums, percussion).

For this unadventurous solo debut Kirwan assembled a band including Andy Silvester and Paul Raymond, formerly of Chicken Shack. Despite their presence, the music doesn't so much as *hint* at Kirwan's blues roots—or come to that, highlight his once-significant guitar work. A singularly uninspired platter, it concentrates on Kirwan's overblown whimsicality. Best ignored.

FLEETWOOD MAC

(A) Rhiannon (Nicks) Stevie Nicks vocal / **(B) Sugar Daddy** (McVie) Christine McVie vocal

Produced: Fleetwood Mac and Keith Olsen. **(US)** Reprise RPS.1345. Released: January 1976. **(UK)** Reprise K.14430. Released: April 1976. Re-released: February 3, 1978.

"Rhiannon," more than any other Mac song, projected Stevie Nicks as a sex symbol. Her first A-side and the one song that instantly established Stevie's earthy seductiveness with The Great American Public. It made her the focal point of the band and gave her that desperately needed shot of confidence.

Those small-time San Francisco promoters weren't wrong after all!

"Rhiannon" is about a schizophrenic Welsh witch. Stevie told one of the authors: "Rhiannon is a good witch. Onstage I really get into the whole character. It's a real mind-tripper. Everybody in the band, especially me, is just blitzed by the end of it. I put out so much of me in that one song that I'm nearly down. There's something about 'Rhiannon' that really connects with a lot of people every time they hear it."

For many, it's Stevie's workout around "Rhiannon" that has made her Linda Ronstadt's closest rival as rock's most desired female star.

Whereas, La Ronstadt plumbs for a more peachy image in her cutoffs and bare midriff, the nubile Nicks prefers more dazzling couture: hip but glamorous. For "Rhiannon," a beguiling opus strung around Buckingham's blurred lower-register guitar riff, Stevie dons diaphanous black chiffon, a silk opera hat and swirls around the stage like something possessed.

Nevertheless, Stevie refutes suggestions of running strictly on a sex appeal ticket: "I'm not terribly aware of that image. I'm pretty naive and gullible." And fears she'll be seen as nothing more than a glorified groupie!

"The last thing I need is to hear one more person saying I'm cute." She is emphatic about wanting to be known for her creativity. "People come up to me every place we play and tell me what an effect 'Rhiannon' has had on their lives. As if it has some spiritual power over them."

The Christine McVie-penned flip, "Sugar Daddy," resurrects her R & B roots as she slips behind a Hammond organ and pulls out the correct stops to duplicate the distinct Booker T choke.

Fleetwood Mac could still get down.

DANNY KIRWAN

(A) Misty River (Kirwan) / **(B) Rolling Hills** (Kirwan)

Produced: Clifford Davis Productions Ltd. **(US)** Not released. **(UK)** DJM DJS.666. Released: May 7, 1976.

Another hopeless attempt at jetting Kirwan into the best sellers. We know there's no potential *Meisterwerks* ensconced within the grooves of Kirwan's second solo LP "Midnight In San Juan," from whence this was extracted, but there were tracks more appropriate for singles release than this largely acoustic doodle. Next . . .

Stevie's rendition of "Rhiannon" made her the rock sex-symbol she is today.

THE ORIGINAL FLEETWOOD MAC–ENGLISH ROSE
FLEETWOOD MAC

Produced: Mike Vernon.
(US) Not released. (UK) CBS 81308-9. Released: June 4, 1976.

Drifting (Green)/**Leaving Town Blues** (Green)/**Watch Out** (Green)/**A Fool No More** (Green)/**Mean Old Fireman** (Trad arr: Spencer)/**Can't Afford To Do It** (Williamson)/**Fleetwood Mac** (Green)/**Worried Dream** (King)/**Love That Woman** (Leake)/**Allow Me One More Show** (Spencer)/**First Train Home** (Green)/**Rambling Pony No. 2** (Green)/**Stop Messin' 'Round** (Green, Adams)/**Jigsaw Puzzle Blues** (Kirwan)/**Doctor Brown** (Brown)/**Something Inside Of Me** (Kirwan)/**Evenin' Boogie** (Spencer)/**Love That Blues** (Green, Adams)/**Black Magic Woman** (Green)/**I've Lost My Baby** (Spencer)/**One Sunny Day**

Above: Of her image as a sex symbol, Stevie says: "I'm not terribly aware of that image. I'm pretty naïve and gullible." Top right: Christine McVie's talent blossomed in the new Mac lineup.

(Kirwan)/**Without You** (Kirwan)/**Coming Home** (James)/**Albatross** (Green)

As the title implies, straight repackage of two vintage albums at budget price.

FLEETWOOD MAC

(A) Say You Love Me (McVie) Christine McVie vocal/**(B) Monday Morning** (Buckingham) Lindsey Buckingham vocal

Produced: Fleetwood Mac and Keith Olsen. (US) Reprise RPS.1356. Released: June 9, 1976. (UK) Reprise K.14447. Released: September 24, 1976.

As if Christine McVie's considerable talent was ever in doubt, "Say You Love Me" encapsulates every aspect of her far-too-often underplayed talent. This hit may have ridden in on the success of "The White Album," but even if Ms. McVie had been a totally unknown artist, "Say You Love Me" would still have split the charts wide open.

A model pop-rock record, it is deftly structured to bring out the very best in both singer and group. The subtle Beatleisms inherent in Buckingham's guitar-harmonics and the about-face "Ticket To Ride" coda add just enough filigree to enhance the song's skeletal arrangement.

The number reflects Christine's self-prognosis that she is "a pretty basic love-song writer." And what, we ask, is so wrong with that?

Obviously, Buckingham's time spent engrossed in his brother's record collection wasn't wasted. Influences fly left, right and center without any particular one being painfully obvious on the B-side's chirpy "Monday Morning."

Like "Rhiannon," "Say You Love Me" was remixed for singles release.

BUCKINGHAM NICKS

(A) Crying In The Night (Nicks)/**(B) Stephanie** (Buckingham)

Produced: Keith Olsen.
Executive Producer: Richard Dashut.
(US) Polydor PD.14335. Released: June 10, 1976. (UK) Not released.

Having long since dumped the by now dynamic duo for having no commercial potential Polydor weren't about to miss out on *curiosity* sales appeal.

The A-side, you already know. The B-side, another Cat Stevens derived finger-pickin' instrumental, was named after you know who! But you know who didn't return the compliment in song.

DANNY KIRWAN

(A) Second Chapter (Kirwan)/**(B) Skip A Dee Doo** (Kirwan)

Produced: Martin Rushent.
(US) DJM DJUS.1014. Released: August 18, 1976. (UK) Not released.

Promo-only copies pressed.

MAC CHANGE THEIR MINDS
Reunion plan shelved

FLEETWOOD MAC have dropped their plan to return permanently to Britain. And this means that the idea of inviting two former members, Peter Green and Danny Kirwan, to re-join the band has also been ditched. But Mac still propose...

the end of August. Their current album "Fleetwood Mac" has now sold over two million copies in America and a single taken from it, "Say You Love Me", will be issued here shortly.

Meanwhile, CBS are this month...

Peter Green to re-join F. Mac?

FLEETWOOD MAC are planning an extensive European tour later this year, and their itinerary will include a string of major concerts in Britain. And there is a distinct possibility of the band returning to an all-British line-up, with guitarist-vocalist Peter Green coming out of retirement to re-join the new-look Mac...

For some strange reason, rumor had it that Mac would take a step back into their bluesy past and add Peter Green (above). It was only a rumor.

The record sleeve for "Go Your Own Way" featured an elegantly attired Mick Fleetwood, and Stevie Nicks in a black diaphanous dress.

FLEETWOOD MAC

(A) Go Your Own Way (Buckingham) Lindsey Buckingham vocal/**(B) Silver Springs** (Nicks) Stevie Nicks vocal

Produced: Fleetwood Mac with Richard Dashut, Ken Caillat, Cris Morris.
(US) Warner Brothers WBS.8304. Released: December 20, 1976. (UK) Warner Brothers K.16872. Released: January 28, 1977. (Limited edition 12-inch promo-only singles pressed: PRO.652)

Like the album that followed it, "Go Your Own Way" showcased Fleetwood Mac—now fueled by success—in a much tougher mood. The band are positively fearsome, slashing out this defiant statement of strength in the face of romantic turbulence—Stevie and Lindsey's five-year relationship had ended.

Could be that like so many artists, Buckingham works best under emotional stress. If his contribution to "The White Album" left something to be desired, "Go Your Own Way" quashes any skepticism about his ability in the studio.

While the fearless Mick Fleetwood and John McVie get to grips to switch the emphasis on the beat, Buckingham uses this rhythm foundation to overdub telling acoustic and electric guitars.

A non-album track, Stevie Nicks' doleful "Silver Springs" reveals that, like her former lover, she too had gained confidence since the last Mac outing. Not only that, Buckingham & Nicks had been totally integrated into The Mac to create a coherent group sound. A passionate and adventurous opus. While Nicks' well-crafted song stands up by itself, the arrangement (Buckingham's?) gives it that added lift.

Christine relaxes at poolside in the California sun.

Prior to the release of "Rumours," personal problems plagued Mac. Christine and John McVie separated; Stevie Nicks and Lindsey Buckingham stopped living together; and Mick Fleetwood realized that his marriage was on the rocks.

RUMOURS
FLEETWOOD MAC

Produced: Fleetwood Mac with Richard Dashut, Ken Caillat, Cris Morris.
(US) Warner Bros BSK.3010. Released: February 4, 1977. (UK) Warner Bros K.56344. Released: February 11, 1977.

Second Hand News (Buckingham) Lindsey Buckingham vocal/**Dreams** (Nicks) Stevie Nicks vocal/**Never Going Back Again** (Buckingham) Lindsey Buckingham vocal/**Don't Stop** (McVie) Christine McVie vocal/**Go Your Own Way** (Buckingham) Lindsey Buckingham vocal/**Songbird** (McVie) Christine McVie vocal/**The Chain** (Buckingham, Nicks, McVie, Fleetwood, McVie) Lindsey Buckingham, Christine McVie, Stevie Nicks vocals/**You Make Loving Fun** (McVie) Christine McVie vocal/**I Don't Want To Know** (Nicks) Lindsey Buckingham, Stevie Nicks vocals/**Oh Daddy** (McVie) Christine McVie vocal/**Gold Dust Woman** (Nicks) Stevie Nicks vocal

Personnel:
Stevie Nicks (vocal), **Lindsey Buckingham** (vocal, guitar), **Christine McVie** (vocal, keyboards), **John McVie** (bass), **Mick Fleetwood** (drums).

Come album time, and you can bank on Fleetwood Mac immersing themselves in all manner of turmoil. Years ago, it would have had a detrimental effect on their music. This time out, Mac refused to allow the fates to tamper with the business at hand.

Even before recording commenced, deep cracks had appeared in the group's personal stability. Over a two-month period Fleetwood Mac's interband love life had plummeted into a nosedive—Christine and John McVie separated halfway through the Buckingham and Nicks inaugural tour, shortly afterward Lindsey and Stevie stopped cohabitating, and Mick Fleetwood, desperately trying to meditate, realized that his marriage was on the skids.

"When the shit hit the fan," said Fleetwood, "everybody thought that this was the end of Fleetwood Mac, and that it would be impossible to work under such intense conditions."

When, in February ('76), the group stumbled into the Sausalito Record Plant to record the followup to "The White Album," the McVies were barely on speaking terms, Buckingham and Nicks' relationship had disintegrated in tears and ill-concealed recriminations, and Mick Fleetwood was in the midst of divorce proceedings.

As Fleetwood recalled, "A helluva bad time to try and record a new album." But out of such a hornet's nest of emotional intrigue was hewn one of the biggest-ever selling rock albums. Fleetwood: "So there we all were trying to put down the basic backing tracks and all feeling desperately unhappy with life. But somehow, things never got bitchy. We created a mutual bond. We could all relate to each other's desperation. And despite ourselves, we refused to lose contact. It wasn't as though there was nobody else to turn to. Strange as it might sound, we had one another. So we went through shit to get to the point where we could still communicate."

To further aggravate the tempestuous atmosphere, the star-crossed lovers were beset with in-studio technical problems. During the nine weeks they were holed up in Sausalito, they not only had to cope with several successive pianos refusing to stay in tune, but also with a recording machine—nicknamed "Jaws"—which had mangled much of what had been recorded.

Stevie Nicks sings in the studio, a study in intensity.

Above: *The March 1977 issue of* Rolling Stone *magazine featured Fleetwood Mac in bed together. Says Mick of the magazine cover: "It wasn't funny at the time." Right: Both Stevie and Christine felt that being with their men day in and day out was partly responsible for their breakups. Here, John McVie concentrates on his music.*

Accustomed to such "inconveniences," Mac resigned themselves to starting afresh. The band traveled south to Miami's Criteria Studios, but the bulk of the outstanding work on "Rumours" was completed in a small studio on Hollywood Boulevard's seamier side. In all, between February and October, Fleetwood Mac spent seven months incarcerated in one studio or another, at a time when all parties concerned wanted to see as little of one another as possible.

"I don't think anyone ever turned round and said, 'I don't need this, I'm splitting,'" revealed Fleetwood. "We all understood how we felt because we were all so involved in each other's lives. It wasn't because of money that we didn't split up the band."

He added, "Sure, we laugh at it now. We even make jokes..." A cover of *Rolling Stone* carried a photograph of all five together in one bed—Christine cuddling Lindsey, Mick with his arm around Stevie and John absorbed in a girlie magazine. "But believe me, it wasn't funny at the time."

Said Stevie, "We were all in pretty bad shape. You know splitting up hasn't been an easy thing for Lindsey and me. I think that deep down we both realized it was the only thing left to do. Neither of us were creating."

Buckingham too can now view the positive side of the split. "The whole breakup forced me to redefine my whole individuality—musically as well. I no longer think of Stevie and myself as a duo. For a time, the thought of going it alone freaked me out. I've fought back to be myself."

Both women in the band partially blame their respective breakups on the claustrophobia of being with their men day in, day out.

Said Christine, "I think I've seen it all. It's really not an easy life. You have to take reasonable care of yourself and be adaptable. Before Stevie joined I was the only girl in the group. I was with John twenty-four hours a day for years and that's why everything went wrong. I had to break up with John for my sanity. If not I'd have ended up in a lunatic asylum."

Fleetwood reiterated Christine's point when he revealed, "The thing that happened between Christine and John and Lindsey and Stevie wasn't that they suddenly took a dislike to one another, they just realized they could no longer live together. So there was no malice. They just fell out of love with one another at the same time.

"Anyway, we'd recorded the backing tracks in nine anxious weeks, but the emotions that we originally put down on tape were so strong that we didn't want to be immature and insensitive toward those feelings. That's why we took so much care in the dubbing and mixing.

"We just went through our collective traumas head-on and it was then that we revealed our true colors. In the past, John and I have had to handle some really weird situations... Peter Green... Jeremy Spencer. But as far as Lindsey and Stevie were concerned they didn't go like lambs to the slaughter. They just underwent a crash course in maturity."

For well over a year Fleetwood Mac supplied America's dirt-diggin' gossip columnists with more Hot Poop than the collective shenanigans of Jackie Onassis, Margaret Trudeau, and Gregg & Cher. If the pundits weren't speculating about Fleetwood Mac's individual sexual preferences, they were

Christine McVie plays and sings in a recent recording session.

The members of the group found their music more rewarding than their personal lives. Their *"Rumours"* album was voted Best Rock Album of the Year.

having a field day ruminating on the group's drug habits. Mick Fleetwood remarrying his ex-wife was, however, regarded as a non-event.

Obviously, sex is an even stronger selling point than death, for as we write, "Rumours" (originally titled "Yesterday's Gone"—a phrase from Christine's "Don't Stop") has sold in excess of 12 million copies worldwide. And still selling.

So why all the fuss?

Mick Fleetwood has his own theories.

"We all felt very strong together. There's a chemistry that I dread to dissect. It's best left alone, otherwise it might ruin something. Not only are the band visually appealing, but when people think of the Eagles or Chicago they just think of a band. When they think of us, they remember real flesh and blood people and not hardened professionals. Musically, with the three singers and the three writers we cover a lot of ground.

"There's a lot of very strong emotional power radiating from Fleetwood Mac; a huge energy exchange between us and an audience. It has nothing to do with music!"

Despite the calamitous conditions under which "Rumours" was laboriously extracted, an aura of spontaneity prevails. One could go so far as to say that it's infused with such invigorating optimism that it belies the collective Mac heartache.

"Rumours" was a cathartic experience with the group expressing their personal snarlups in song. Despite the witless lyrics, neither Buckingham, Nicks or McVie degenerate into self-indulgence, mawkish sentimentality or, God-forbid, wimpishness. Rather, they sound vibrant and resilient.

A downer, "Rumours" is not.

Keith Olsen—the producer of "The White Album"—is conspicuous by his absence. Instead, Fleetwood Mac themselves produce the album with the assistance of three engineers. Fleetwood stated that unlike "The White Album," "Rumours" was "felt out and not executed." A cursory listen confirms his opinion.

Unlike its predecessor, "Rumours" boasts a three-dimensional sound quality, and one that's been expertly mixed to fully emphasize the almost majestic deployment of both instruments and voices. In fact, the technical expertise of this album has received as many industry award nominations as the actual performance.

In the very best pop traditions, the arrangements are imaginative without being overblown. If on "The White Album" Fleetwood Mac had adopted for the first time a collective strategy in interpreting one another's material, on "Rumours" they go one better. The devastating vocal harmonies are arranged with such skill that no matter who takes lead, the remaining voices are shuffled to produce an overall distinctive sound, neither routine nor bland.

This is matched with instrumental prowess. Lindsey Buckingham and Mick Fleetwood are to be particularly saluted in this context. For the first time on record Buckingham has taken his innumerable influences and, with taste and sensitivity, personalized them. His guitar work is meticulous and spirited. One feels it is not overzealous to draw parallels between Buckingham's work on "Rumours" and George Harrison's contributions to "Rubber Soul" and "Revolver." Witness the corkscrewed coiffured one's attractive guitar inflections on "Second Hand News," "Dreams" and "You Make Loving Fun." His solos are purposeful and, like the rest of the instrumentation, always economical.

It's difficult to think of another group album where the drummer plays such an important role without ripping off his T-shirt, smothering the kit in smoke bombs, and hogging the limelight. Fleetwood is the centrifugal force of Mac's predominant hard-rock focus. He's imaginative without being flash. He also looks cute in a dress....

In contrast, John McVie is felt more than heard. Yet Fleetwood without McVie would be like Laurel without Hardy.

To American rock audiences, Fleetwood Mac have emerged as the most easily identifiable personalities since the demise of a group of four blokes we refuse to mention. Fleetwood and McVie are the group's Odd Couple. Buckingham—the well-to-do All-American whiz-kid who couldn't have done better unless he'd been a peanut farmer.

Nicks and McVie clown for a photographer.

Christine and Stevie confirm that gentlemen *do* prefer blondes. Chistine is at once Big Sister and Earth Mother; Stevie is fast becoming a media cult figure, responsible for much of "Rumours" impact in the same way as Farrah Fawcett-Majors trebled the sale of electric curling tongs.

While Mac's lovelorn vignettes are not dripping with hooks, these songs evince an insidious quality which doesn't pale with persistent plays. It's the subtlety of the melodies that's kept most of the songs, when released as singles, habitually on the world's playlists. That subtlety is the prime reason why, nearly a year after its release, "Rumours" was still selling 250,000 every week.

A flawless album, for which Fleetwood Mac have harvested practically every award possible for any rock band to scoop. If they chose to release the hole in the middle, that too would probably go double-platinum....

FLEETWOOD MAC

(A) Dreams (Nicks) Stevie Nicks vocal/**(B) Song-bird** (McVie) Christine McVie vocal

Produced: Fleetwood Mac with Richard Dashut, Ken Caillat, Cris Morris.
(US) Warner Bros WBS.8371. Released: April 4, 1977. (UK) Warner Bros K.16969. Released: June 17, 1977.

Another statement from Mac's album of internal conversations about their romantic trials, "Dreams" can be viewed as Stevie's reply to Lindsey's "Go Your Own Way." Whereas Lindsey sounded downright volatile, Nicks adopts a more stealthy tack. Talk about

John McVie seems oblivious to both cameras and audience as he communicates with his guitar during a concert.

Lindsey Buckingham, enjoying himself during a recent concert.

a "I can't live with you, can't live without you" situation!

Though "Dreams" clocks in at over four minutes, it's a measure of Stevie's artistic development that the long-drawn-out melody line (only punctuated by the chorus) doesn't become tedious. Mark the sheer subtlety of the arrangement which allows the song to grow at its own pace.

On "Songbird"—recorded live at Zeller-back Auditorium, U.C. Berkeley—Christine wears her heart on her sleeve. A reflective, austere point number, it shows the Mac aren't afraid to sometimes stand naked.

"I don't like to hear it all that much," Christine revealed about this poignant lover's lament.

MIDNIGHT IN SAN JUAN
DANNY KIRWAN

Produced: Clifford Davis Productions Ltd.
(US) DJM DJL.PA9. Released: May 9, 1977.
(UK) DJM DJF.20481. Released: September 9, 1976.

I Can Tell (Kirwan)/Life Machine (Kirwan)/Midnight In San Juan (Kirwan)/Let It Be (Lennon, McCartney)/Angel's Delight (Kirwan)/Windy Autumn Day (Kirwan)/Misty River (Kirwan)/Rolling Hills (Kirwan)/I Can't Let You Go (Kirwan)/Look Around You (Kirwan)/Castaway (Kirwan)

Personnel:
Danny Kirwan (vocal, guitars), John Cook (piano), Steve Emery (bass), Jeff Rich (drums).

Though better than its predecessor, what decent song ideas there are fail to make anything other than the slightest impression by dint of Kirwan's limp backup musicians and a production job which does him no justice at all. Interviewed at the time by one of the authors, Kirwan was—to say the least—hardly on the ball. It is hoped that at some point in the future Kirwan will—as they say—get his head together and sign with a label who know how to maximize his talent. Where are you, Mick Fleetwood?

FLEETWOOD MAC

(A) Don't Stop (McVie) Christine McVie vocal/(B) Gold Dust Woman (Nicks) Stevie Nicks vocal

Produced: Fleetwood Mac with Richard Dashut, Ken Caillat, Cris Morris.
(US) Not released. (UK) Warner Bros K.16930.
Released: April 1, 1977.

As ever, Mick Fleetwood's nigh-on peerless snare drum propels that group into overdrive on this streamlined Christine McVie shuffle. While perhaps not one of her best songs, the high-energy groove sustains, and "Don't Stop" comes into its own with its obvious crowd-pleasing get-'em-up-and-in-the-aisles pizazz. A paean to optimism, "Don't Stop" was doubtless inspired in an attempt at self-consolation after her breakup with John.

Written in a minor key, "Gold Dust Woman," rekindles visions of "Rhiannon," but on this occasion Stevie fixes her attention on groupies and not celtic folklore.

She said: "It's about women who stand around and give me and Christine dirty looks, but as soon as a guy comes in the room are overcome with smiles."

DANNY KIRWAN

(A) Hot Summer's Day (Kirwan)/**(B) Love Can Always Bring You Happiness** (Kirwan)

Produced: Martin Rushent.
(US) Not released. (UK) DJM DJS.10783. Released: June 7, 1977.

Purely perfunctory release from DJM who seem baffled by Kirwan's out-of-focus talent. Hardly arresting.

FLEETWOOD MAC

(A) Don't Stop (McVie) Christine McVie vocal/**(B) Never Going Back Again** (Buckingham) Lindsey Buckingham vocal

Produced: Fleetwood Mac with Richard Dashut, Ken Caillat, Cris Morris.
(US) Warner Bros WBS.8413. Released: July 6, 1977. (UK) Not released.

Just to make life difficult, America reshuffles the B-sides.

Mick Fleetwood's superlative drumming was one of the high points on the Mac single "Don't Stop."

Green committed

APPEARING UNDER his real name of Peter Greenbaum, former Fleetwood Mac guitarist Peter Green (30) was last Wednesday, at Marylebone Court, committed for treatment at a mental hospital.

This followed an incident last month when Green was arrested following a row with accountant Clifford Adams at his Westbourne Park address over Green's demands that royalty payments from his hit records be stopped. Amounts involved are in the region of £30,000-a-year.

Green admitted having a pump-action rifle without a firearms certificate, but denied threatening to damage windows at Adams' West End offices.

In his defence David Bray told the court that since his client left the group in 1971, "it appears there has been some difficulties . . . and his

CHRIS SALEWICZ details the sad story of PETER GREEN, which last week culminated in a court-order committing him to mental hospital . . .

attitude is that he wishes to make his own way through life rather than make use of any royalties from his past records."

Making the hospital order Sir Ivor Rigby told Green: "I hope you understand that I am really only interested in trying to help you."

SINCE GREEN decided to quit

The sad story of Peter Green's difficulties since leaving F.M. is all too common in the music business.

ALBATROSS—FLEETWOOD MAC & CHRISTINE PERFECT
FLEETWOOD MAC—CHRISTINE PERFECT

Produced: *Mike Vernon. **Mike Vernon and Christine Perfect. ***Danny Kirwan. (US) Not released. (UK) CBS-Embassy 31569. Released: August 5, 1977.

FLEETWOOD MAC: *Albatross (Green)/* Rambling Pony (Green)/*I Believe My Time Ain't Long (Spencer)/*Doctor Brown (Brown)/*Stop Messin' 'Round (Green, Adams)/ *Love That Burns (Green, Adams)/*Jigsaw Puzzle Blues (Kirwan)/*Need Your Love Tonight (Spencer)

CHRISTINE PERFECT: **I'd Rather Go Blind (Jordan, Foster)/**Crazy 'Bout You Baby (Williamson)/**And That's Saying A Lot (Jackson, Godfrey)/**I'm On My Way (Malone)/**No Road Is The Right Road (Perfect)/**Let Me Go (Leave Me Alone) (Perfect)/**I'm Too Far Gone (To Turn Around) (Otis, Hendricks)/***When You Say (Kirwan)

The Mac tracks proliferate on many still-in-print compilations. If they were so bothered to dig out Christine's skeleton in the cupboard, why only include two-thirds of her old material? Come to think of it, why bother at all?

DANNY KIRWAN

(A) Let It Be (Lennon, McCartney)/(B) I Can Tell (Kirwan)

Produced: Clifford Davis Productions Ltd. (US) DJM DJUS.1025. Released: August 1977. (UK) Not released.

Yes, Fab Paul's Holy Ballad, here given a "toy" reggae rendition. Neither the former Beatle nor Bob Marley need lose any sleep.

THE HISTORY OF FLEETWOOD MAC—VINTAGE YEARS
FLEETWOOD MAC

Produced: Mike Vernon.
(US) Sire 2XS.6006. Released: September 16, 1977. (UK) CBS 88227. Released: March 4, 1977.

Black Magic Woman (Green)/Coming Home (James)/Rambling Pony (Green)/Something Inside Of Me (Kirwan)/Dust My Broom (James)/ The Sun Is Shining (James)/Albatross (Green)/ *Just The Blues (Boyd)/Evenin' Boogie (Spencer) /*The Big Boat (Boyd)/Jigsaw Puzzle Blues (Kirwan)/I've Lost My Baby (Spencer)/Doctor Brown (Brown)/Need Your Love So Bad (John)/ Looking For Somebody (Green)/Need Your Love Tonight (Spencer)/Shake Your Moneymaker (James)/Man Of The World (Green)/Stop Messin' 'Round (Green, Adams)/Rollin' Man (Green, Adams)/Love That Burns (Green, Adams) /If You Be My Baby (Green, Adams)/Lazy Poker Blues (Green, Adams)/Trying So Hard To Forget (Green, Adams) *features Eddie Boyd (vocal, piano)

A straight pre-'70 reissue job.

Lindsey Buckingham plays a solo during a recent concert.

Stevie Nicks and Rod Stewart trade quips and yarns at a West Coast party.

FRENCH KISS
BOB WELCH

Produced: John Carter. *Lindsey Buckingham and Christine McVie.
(US) Capitol ST.11663. Released: September 12, 1977. (UK) Capitol CL.15951. Released: November 18, 1977.

*Sentimental Lady (Welch)/Easy To Fall (Welch)/Hot Love, Cold World (Welch, Henning)/Mystery Train (Welch)/Lose My Heart (Welch)/Outskirts (Welch, Carter)/Ebony Eyes (Welch)/Lose Your (Welch)/Carolene (Welch)/Dancin' Eyes (Welch)/Danchiva (Welch)/Lose Your Heart (Welch)

Personnel:
Bob Welch (vocal, guitars, bass), Alvin Taylor (drums), *Bob Welch (vocal, bass), Christine McVie (vocal, keyboards), Lindsey Buckingham (vocal, guitar, arranger), Mick Fleetwood (drums).

Though between April 1971 and December 1974, Bob Welch contributed 20 originals to the Fleetwood Mac archives, collaborating on another three, he offered no real indication that he would eventually mature to conceive and produce a solo album of this undisputed excellence.

In between leaving Mac and cutting this album, Welch maintained a very low profile (apart from appearing as a guest on Bill Wyman's "Stone Alone" LP) until he re-emerged in January 1976, the leader of Paris, a glitzy power trio which included former Jethro Tull bassist Glenn Cornick and Nazz drummer Thom Mooney; the latter later replaced by the Iggy Pop drummer Hunt Sales.

After leaving Mac,
Bob Welch didn't reappear on the music scene until 1976.

Top: *Mick Fleetwood.* Bottom: *Stevie Nicks relaxes between takes.*

Paris cut two albums for Capitol, but fell between too many stools and dissolved through lack of management, direction, and work. "With," says Welch, "a whimper, not a bang."

Originally, Welch, with a new manager in tow, intended to move to New York where he would front a larger rock 'n' boogie outfit. But the project was stillborn, and Welch easily persuaded Capitol to underwrite this solo album. His former colleague Mick Fleetwood, having proven his capabilities as Mac's manager, shortly afterwards took on the additional responsibility of being Welch's manager.

Stronger than anything Welch produced for the Fleetwood Mac Songbook, the effervescent "French Kiss" may slip perfectly into the current, highly lucrative Hip Easy Listening category, yet it easily transcends the one-dimensional blandness that genre often evokes.

"French Kiss" is primarily a quality pop-rock radio album bursting with singles potential, and comparable to the very best aspects of Mac's "White Album" and "Rumours." Despite its genetic connections, it shouldn't be viewed as a surrogate Mac album and wasn't promoted as such.

If the material is excellent, then the production (John Carter) and the performance (apart from drummer Alvin Taylor, Welch plays all instruments, except on "Sentimental Lady" where he's augmented by all of Fleetwood Mac, save for Stevie Nicks and John McVie) are equally important to the success of "French Kiss."

Having scaled the heights of the American best sellers with mercurial speed, Bob Welch's immediate prospects seem ensured. In February 1978, he commenced his first American solo tour—backed by a band handpicked by Fleetwood and himself—and looked after by Fleetwood Mac's road crew.

FLEETWOOD MAC

(A) You Make Loving Fun (McVie) Christine McVie vocal/**(B) Never Going Back** (Buckingham) Lindsey Buckingham vocal

Produced: Fleetwood Mac with Richard Dashut, Ken Caillat, Cris Morris.
(US) Not released. (UK) Warner Brothers K.17013. Released: September 16, 1977.

Fleetwood Mac's founder members may have co-opted a couple of seemingly incongruous Californian Sunkist Kids into their ranks, but the original British contingent haven't deviated from their roots.

"You Make Loving Fun," underpinned with tastefully mixed electric keyboards, is R & B as Fleetwood and the McVies choose to interpret it. As expected, they don't sell themselves short in the process. Even with so many voices now in the band, it's not easy to ignore the rhythm section—their excellence should never for one moment be overlooked.

Buckingham's sinuous guitar solo is exemplary, as are his fills, a synthesis of West Coast ideas and traditional British rock stylistic devices.

The B-side shows that Buckingham has still to let his membership to the Cat Stevens Fan Club lapse. While Buckingham's attributes as a guitarist and arranger have improved beyond all recognition, his songwriting, particularly in this style, still has its lapses of taste.

FLEETWOOD MAC

(A) Go Your Own Way (Buckingham) Lindsey Buckingham vocal/**(B) Dreams** (Nicks) Stevie Nicks vocal

Produced: Fleetwood Mac with Richard Dashut, Ken Caillat, Cris Morris.
(US) Warner Bros GWB.0348. Released: September 23, 1977. (UK) Not released.

The first two A-sides extracted from "Rumours," rapidly re-pressed as instant "Golden Oldies."

BOB WELCH

(A) *Sentimental Lady (Welch)/**(B) **Hot Love, Cold World** (Welch, Henning)

Produced: *Lindsey Buckingham and Christine McVie. **John Carter..
(US) Capitol 44779. Released: October 3, 1977. (UK) Not released.

"Sentimental Lady" was first released as a single by Fleetwood Mac in May 1972. For the next four years Warners promotion team, convinced of the song's commerciality, annually reserviced the media with copies of this record hoping to prove their point.

Mick Fleetwood too was convinced that "Sentimental Lady" had chartability. At his suggestion, Welch recut the song, this time with a more sophisticated arrangement—courtesy of Lindsey Buckingham.

Welch sings lead and plays bass. Fleetwood drums, while Christine McVie and Buckingham supply vocal backup, and keyboards and guitars respectively.

It went Top 20.

FLEETWOOD MAC

(A) You Make Loving Fun (McVie) Christine McVie vocal/**(B) Gold Dust Woman** (Nicks) Stevie Nicks vocal

Produced: Fleetwood Mac with Richard Dashut, Ken Caillat, Cris Morris.
(US) Warner Bros WBS.8483. Released: October 5, 1977. (UK) Not released.

For the States, the British B-side of "Don't Stop" was picked.

BOB WELCH

(A) Ebony Eyes (Welch)/**(B) Dancin' Eyes** (Welch)

Produced: John Carter.
(US) Capitol 4543. Released: February 1978. (UK) Capitol 15951. Released: November 4, 1977.

Not to be confused with The Everly Brothers' 1961 hit of the same name, "Ebony Eyes" picked up maximum British radio airtime, but still narrowly missed the Top 30. Perhaps, if more people had seen the bizarre high-budget promo clip featuring the exquisite young damsel, handcuffed to an Arab, to whom Welch addresses the song, it would have been a different story.

A crisp uptempo pelvic pulsation, spliced with Welch's abrupt guitar figures, taut disco flash from drummer Alvin Taylor, and brisk strings, "Ebony Eyes" confirms that Bob Welch had found his niche at last.

Stateside, "Outskirts" was chosen as its flip.

Top: *John McVie.* Bottom: *Christine McVie belts out a song during a recent concert.*

The Mac today.

At the time of writing, Fleetwood Mac are scheduling sessions for a new album—a projected double. Also, they are contemplating their summer 1978 plans to tour Russia, which ought to be a much-publicized affair (though their attempts at interesting a major television network in covering the goodwill concert tour from start to finish seemed to have fizzled out).

They are continuing to reap awards. In December 1977, *Rolling Stone* chose "Rumours" as one of the albums of the year, saying: "Not because 'Rumours' was the best selling album of the year, but because it may well have been the best...from the diversity of the writing and singing to the punch of the rhythm section, it's impossible not to think of the Beatles."

Barely two months following the rock magazine's accolades, Fleetwood Mac's "Rumours" garnered yet another Grammy award, for "Best Album of the Year."

Peter Green has miraculously resurfaced. In early February 1978, it was announced that Green had signed with PVK Records, an obscure British label, and there is talk of Mick Fleetwood producing and managing his former colleague.

Jeremy Spencer has moved from South America to Italy where, according to eye-witnesses, he has formed an Anglo–American band, demoed some new material, and is planning a re-entry into the music business.

Danny Kirwan is keeping a low profile, and it is alleged that he is label-less.

Far left: *Peter Green has recently reemerged into the music world, having signed a contract with a small record company.* Left: *Jeremy Spencer is currently living in Italy and plans to form his own group there.* Above: *After choosing "Rumours" as the Best-Selling Album of the Year, Rolling Stone magazine featured Fleetwood Mac on their cover.*

The discography below includes recordings by artists and groups wherein Fleetwood Mac members were involved. Albums are listed in all upper case letters; singles are listed in upper and lower case.

BO STREET RUNNERS

Baby Never Say Goodbye/Get Out Of My Way
(US) Not released. (UK) Columbia DB.7640. Released: July 1965.
Produced: No credit.

THE CHEYNES

Respectable/It's Gonna Happen To You
(US) Not released. (UK) Columbia DB.7153. Released: December 1963.
Produced: No credit.

Goin' To The River/Cheyne-Re-La
(US) Not released. (UK) Columbia DB.7386. Released: October 1964.
Produced: No credit.

Down And Out/Stop Running Around
(US) Not released. (UK) Columbia DB.7464. Released: February 1965.
Produced: No credit.

CLIFFORD DAVIS

(Manager Clifford Davis supplying Peter Green-inspired vocals and strings over remixed Fleetwood Mac backing tracks.)

Before The Beginning/Man Of The World
(US) Not released. (UK) Reprise RS 27003. Released: October 1969.
Produced: Clifford Davis.

Come On Down And Follow Me/Homework
(US) Not released. (UK) Reprise 27008. Released: July 1970.
Produced: Clifford Davis.

Man Of The World/Before The Beginning
(US) Not released. (UK) Reprise K.14282. Released: July 1973.
Produced: Clifford Davis.

WALTER EGAN

FUNDAMENTAL ROLE
(US) CBS PC.34679. Released: March 1977. (UK) United Artists UAG.30032. Released: May 1977.
Produced: Lindsey Buckingham, Stevie Nicks, Duane Scott, Walter Egan
Songs: Only The Lucky[1,4]/Won't You Say You Will[1,4]/Waitin'[1,2]/Feel So Good[1,3]/Yes I Guess I Am[1,3]/When I Get My Wheels[4]/Where's The Party[1,2]/She's So Tough/Tunnel O'Love[1,3]/I'd Rather Have Fun[1,2]/Surfin' And Drivin'[1,2]
The above tracks feature:
[1]Lindsey Buckingham (guitar)
[2]Lindsey Buckingham (backing vocals)
[3]Stevie Nicks (backing vocals)
[4]Lindsey Buckingham & Stevie Nicks (backing vocals)

The following tracks were issued as singles:
Only The Lucky/I'd Rather Have Fun
(US) CBS 3-10531. Released: February 10, 1977.
(UK) United Artists UP.36245. Released: April.1, 1977.
When I Get My Wheels/Waitin'
(US) CBS 310591. Released: July 19, 1977. (UK) United Artists UP.36321. Released: October 21, 1977.

ALVIN LEE & MYLON LeFEVRE

*So Sad (No Love Of His Own)/Riffin'
(US) Columbia 45987. Released: December 17, 1973.
(UK) Chrysalis CHS.2035. Released: April 19, 1974.
Produced: Alvin Lee.
Personnel: *Mylon LeFevre (vocal), George Harrison (guitar, slide guitar, bass, vocals), Alvin Lee (guitar, vocal), Ron Wood (12-string guitar), Mick Fleetwood (drums).

Tracks also included on:
ON THE ROAD TO FREEDOM
(US) Columbia KC.32729. Released: December 7, 1973.
(UK) Chrysalis CHR.1054. Released: November 2, 1973.

JOHN MAYALL'S BLUESBREAKERS

(British discography)

Crawling Up A Hill/Mr. James
Decca F.11900.
Produced: Mike Vernon. Released: May 1964.
Personnel: John Mayall (vocal, harmonica, keyboards), Bernie Watson (guitar), John McVie (bass), Martin Hart (drums).

JOHN MAYALL PLAYS JOHN MAYALL
Decca LK.4680.
Produced: Tony Clarke. Released: March 1965.
Personnel: John Mayall (vocal, harmonica, cembalett, organ, guitar), Roger Dean (guitar), John McVie (bass), Hughie Flint (drums), Nigel Stanger (saxes).

Crocodile Walk/Blues City Shakedown
Decca F.12120.
Produced: Mike Vernon. Released: April 1965.
Personnel: John Mayall (vocal, harmonica, keyboards), Roger Dean (guitar), John McVie (bass), Hughie Flint (drums).

I'm Your Witchdoctor/Telephone Blues
Immediate 012.
Produced: Jimmy Page. Released: September 1965.
Personnel: John Mayall (vocal, keyboards, harmonica), Eric Clapton (guitar), John McVie (bass), Hughie Flint (drums).

BLUESBREAKERS WITH ERIC CLAPTON
Decca LK.4804.
Produced: Mike Vernon. Released: May 1966.
Personnel: John Mayall (vocal, keyboards, harmonica), Eric Clapton (vocal, guitar), John McVie (bass), Hughie Flint (drums), Alan Skidmore, John Almond (saxes), Dennis Healey (trumpet).

Parchman Farm/Key To Love
Decca F.12490.
Produced: Mike Vernon. Released: September 1966.
Personnel: same as "Bluesbreakers" LP.

Looking Back/So Many Roads
Decca F.12506.
Produced: Mike Vernon. Released: October 1966.
Personnel: John Mayall (vocal, keyboards, guitar, harmonica), Peter Green (guitar), John McVie (bass), Aynsley Dunbar (drums).

Sitting In The Rain/Out Of Reach
Decca F.12545.
Produced: Mike Vernon. Released: January 1967.
Personnel: John Mayall (vocal, keyboards, guitar, harmonica), Peter Green (vocal, guitar), John McVie (bass), Aynsley Dunbar (drums).

A HARD ROAD
Decca SKL.4853.
Produced: Mike Vernon. Released: February 1967.
Personnel: John Mayall (vocal, guitar, keyboards, harmonica), Peter Green (vocal, guitar), John McVie (bass), Aynsley Dunbar (drums), John Almond, Alan Skidmore, Ray Warleigh (saxes).

Curly/Rubber Duck
Decca F.12588.
Produced: Mike Vernon. Released: March 1967.
Personnel: Peter Green (guitar), John McVie (bass), Aynsley Dunbar (drums).

Double Trouble/It Hurts Me Too
Decca F.12621.
Produced: Mike Vernon. Released: June 1967.
Personnel: John Mayall (vocal, keyboards, guitar), Peter Green (guitar), John McVie (bass), Mick Fleetwood (drums).

JOHN MAYALL'S BLUESBREAKERS WITH PAUL BUTTERFIELD

Decca DFE-R.8673.
Produced: Mike Vernon. Released: April 1967.
Personnel: John Mayall (vocal, keyboards, harmonica), Paul Butterfield (vocal, harmonica), John McVie (bass), Mick Fleetwood (drums).

CRUSADE
Decca LK.4890.
Produced: Mike Vernon. Released: September 1967.
Personnel: John Mayall (vocal, guitar, harmonica, keyboards), Mick Taylor (guitar), John McVie (bass), Keef Hartley (drums), Rip Kant (saxes).

THRU THE YEARS
Decca SKL.5086.
Produced: Mike Vernon. Released: October 1971.
Personnel: John Mayall (vocal, guitar, harmonica, keyboards), Peter Green or Roger Dean or Bernie Watson (guitars), John McVie (bass), Hughie Flint or Martin Hart or Aynsley Dunbar (drums).

PARIS

PARIS
(US) Capitol ST.11464. Released: January 1976.
(UK) Capitol ST.11464. Released: May 1976.
Produced: Jimmy Robinson
Songs: Black Book/Religion/Starcage/Beautiful Youth/Nazarene/Narrow Gate (La Porte Etroite)/Solitaire/Breathless/Rock Of Ages/Red Rain
Personnel: Robert Welch (vocal, guitar), Glenn Cornick (bass, keyboards), Thom Mooney (drums).

BIG TOWNE, 2061
(US) Capitol ST.11560. Released: August 1976.
(UK) Capitol ST.11560. Released: December 1976.
Produced: Bob Hughes
Songs: Blue Robin/Big Towne/Pale Horse, Pale Rider/New Orleans/Outlaw Game/Money Love/Heart Of Stone/Slave Trader/1 in 10/Janie
Personnel: Robert Welch (vocal, guitar), Glenn Cornick (bass, keyboards), Hunt Sales (vocal, drums).

PARIS
Big Towne, 2061/Blue Robin
(US) Capitol 4356. Released: November 1976.
(UK) Not released.
Produced: Bob Hughes

PETER B'S LOONERS

If You Wanna Be Happy/Jodrell Blues
(US) Not released. (UK) Columbia DB.7862. Released: March 1966.
Produced: No credit.

THE SHOTGUN EXPRESS

I Could Feel The Whole World Turn Round/Curtains
(US) Not released. (UK) Columbia DB.8025. Released: October 1966.
Produced: No credit.

Funny 'Cos Neither Could I/Indian Thing
(US) Not released. (UK) Columbia DB.8178. Released: February 1967.
Produced: No credit.

WARREN ZEVON

WARREN ZEVON
(US) Asylum 7E-1060. Released: May 1976.
(UK) Asylum K.53039. Released: May 1976.
Produced: Jackson Browne
Songs: Frank And Jesse James/Mama Couldn't Be Persuaded/*Backs Turned Looking Down The Path/Hasten Down The Wind/**Poor Poor Pitiful Me/The French Inhaler/***Mohammed's Radio/I'll Sleep When I'm Dead/Carmelita/Join Me In L.A./Desperados Under The Eaves
The above tracks feature:
  *Lindsey Buckingham (guitar)
  **Lindsey Buckingham (vocal harmonies)
  ***Lindsey Buckingham & Stevie Nicks (vocal harmonies)

The following tracks were issued as singles:
Hasten Down The Wind/Mohammed's Radio
(US) Asylum E.45356. Released: November 9, 1976.
I'll Sleep When I'm Dead/Mohammed's Radio
(UK) Asylum K.13060. Released: October 8, 1976.

EXCITABLE BOY
(US) Asylum 6E-118. Released: February 1978.
(UK) Asylum K.53073. Released: March 1978.
Produced: Jackson Browne
Songs: Johnny Strikes Up The Band/Excitable Boy/Roland The Headless Thompson Gunner/*Werewolves Of London/Accidentally Like A Martyr/Nighttime In The Switching Yard/Veracruz/Tenderness On The Block/Lawyers, Guns And Money
***The above tracks feature:**
John McVie (bass) & Mick Fleetwood (drums).

BOOTLEGS RECORDS

THE ROCKHOPPERS LIVE.
Songs: Station Man/Spare Me A Little/Rhiannon/
Landslide/I'm So Afraid/World Turning/Don't Let Me
Down Again/Hypnotized.

WILL THE REAL FLEETWOOD MAC PLEASE STAND UP?
Songs: The Green Manalishi/Angel/Spare Me A
Little/Sentimental Lady/Future Games/The Bermuda
Triangle/Why/Believe Me/Black Magic Woman/Oh
Well/Cliff Davis Blooze/Rattle Snake Shake/
Hypnotized.

PICK UP A PENGUIN—STAY ON TOP.
Songs: Station Man/Don't Let Me Down Again/
Rhiannon/Don't Stop/Dreams/Oh Well/The Chain/
Never Going Back Again/Second Hand News/Over
My Head/Say You Love Me/Go Your Own Way/Blue
Letter.

PORTMANTEAU
Songs: (Recorded at The Santa Monica Civic Auditorium 1968.) Rattlesnake Shake/Underway/Tiger/The
Green Manalishi.
(Recorded at BBC Broadcast, London, 1970.) Station
Man/Tell Me All The Things You Do.

ROY CARR

A well-known music journalist, Roy Carr is the Special Projects Editor of London's *New Musical Express*, the world's most prestigious and influential music weekly.

Before turning writer, Carr was a professional musician intimately connected with the "sweaty side" of the music world and has a two-million-record sale to his credit. Carr is also the coauthor of two highly successful books, *The Rolling Stones: An Illustrated Record* and *The Beatles: An Illustrated Record*.

STEVE CLARKE

Obsessed with rock music from an early age, Steve Clark has worked as a staff writer for *New Musical Express* for the past five years. He has also written for various U.S. publications, including *Creem* and *Rolling Stone*, and is the author of a book about Peter Frampton.